William James Henderson

Sea Yarns for Boys

William James Henderson

Sea Yarns for Boys

ISBN/EAN: 9783744718646

Printed in Europe, USA, Canada, Australia, Japan

Cover: Foto ©Andreas Hilbeck / pixelio.de

More available books at **www.hansebooks.com**

[Page 181

"'THE BLOOMIN' SHARK WENT HEAD-FUST INTO THE HOLE'"

SEA YARNS FOR BOYS

Spun by an Old Salt

BY

W. J. HENDERSON

ILLUSTRATED

NEW YORK

HARPER & BROTHERS PUBLISHERS

1895

TO

MY ESTEEMED SHIPMATE

THEODORE C. ZEREGA

CONTENTS

ILLUSTRATIONS

THE Old Sailor sat on the outer end of the pier and looked out over the waves. Henry Hovey and his brother George stood on the inner end of the pier and looked at the Old Sailor. They knew he was an Old Sailor because they had been told so; but he did not wear a blue shirt with a rolling collar with anchors embroidered on it, nor a flat-crowned cap without a brim, nor wide trousers. He wore a fur cap, a short coat of rough material, and his brown trousers were tucked into his boot-legs. But their mother had said he was an Old Sailor who had left the sea and had come there to live in peace the remainder of his days.

"I wonder if he would tell us a yarn?" said George.

"That's a good idea," said Henry. "Suppose we try him."

They walked out to the end of the pier, and rather timidly approached the Old Sailor.

"How are ye, lads?" was his greeting. "It's a putty day, if ye like the wind."

"Yes, sir," said George; "it is a pretty day, and I like the wind quite well."

1

"If you please, Mr. Old Sailor," said Henry, "will you tell us a yarn?"

"Wot kind of a yarn?" asked the Old Sailor, looking at Henry suspiciously.

"Why, a sailor's yarn—something about the sea."

The Old Sailor scanned the horizon, and laughed quietly to himself. "I wonder who gave 'em the course," he muttered.

Henry and George looked at one another anxiously. They did not know what to make of the Old Sailor's manner. Presently he looked around at the boys, and, pointing out to sea, said:

"S'posin'—now mind, I don't say as I do—but s'posin' I was to go fur to ask you wot kind of a wessel was that un, wot 'd you say?"

"A bark," answered both boys, promptly.

"That's werry good, too. An' s'posin' I was to go so fur as to ask you wot was the name o' the sail that sticks out behind, wot 'd you say?"

"Spanker," the answer came.

"That's more'n werry good. An' s'posin' I was to go some further an' ask you about wot course she might be steerin', wot 'd you say?"

"North," said Henry, doubtfully.

"Northeast, is not it?" said George.

"Not so werry good," answered the Old Sailor, again laughing one of his hearty but quiet laughs.

"Waal, then," he broke out suddenly, "you may call me a farmer if this wasn't the way of it. I'd ben an' shipped on a bark called the *Central Park*, bound from Noo Yawk to San Sebastian with a cargo o' spectacles an' guinea-pigs. You see, all the people in San Sebastian are near-sighted, an' have to wear spectacles, an' their favorite sport is guinea-pig races. Them there guinea-pigs was the liveliest set o' quadrupeds wot you ever see, an' the boys took a likin' to 'em an' started in to teach 'em to chaw terbaccer, so's they'd behave theirselves like gen'lemen aboard ship. But the old man—that's the capt'n, you know — stopped that, 'cos he said it 'd put the pigs out o' trainin' for their races at San Seb. Howsumever, that ain't neither here nor there, seein' as how it 'ain't got nothin' to do with this 'ere yarn wot I'm a-tellin' you.

"The *Central Park* was one o' the gallusest old hookers wot I ever sailed on, an' I ben to sea, man an' boy, for more'n forty years. She had a bowsprit half as long as her hull, an' a jib-boom as long as the rest of it, an' it riz up in front o' her like a big pug-nose. When a man was out on the end o' that jib-boom an' the bark riz up on a good sea, he could see right over the tops o' the masts an' down into the cabin door; if he couldn't, I'm a farmer. But that ain't neither here nor there, seein' as how it 'ain't got nothin' to do with this 'ere yarn wot I'm a-tellin' you.

"The *Central Park* were a good-sized barky, an' she carried double tops, wot wasn't so usual in them days, an' had a spanker as big as the mainsail of a yacht. She were a wall-sided old gal, an' w'en you looked over the bulwarks, it were like squintin' down the side of a four-story house. She could sail ten knots an hour in half a breeze a wind, an' I've heerd tell as how she could make sixteen in a hurricane; but I don't know nothin' about that, 'cos she never went at no half-way gait like that when I was aboard. She were allus driftin' or goin' like a express train.

"Waal, the spectacles were stowed in the hold, an' the guinea-pigs between decks. Everything were werry comf'table—werry comf'table indeed— an' we was a-havin' the prettiest kind o' weather, till we was eighteen days out, w'en we was in latitude 92° 15′ north and longitude 206° 15′ west, which, as everybody knows, is just half-way between Coney Island an' San Seb. It were a dead-an'-buried calm, an' I were at the wheel. Our course were east-southeast, an' nothin' off; but as we was a-driftin', I didn't have nothin' to do 'cept to keep the wheel from turnin' flip-flops w'en the ole gal fell down off the swells. The watch was a-lyin' 'round the deck half asleep in the b'ilin' sun, an' the air were hotter'n a bake-oven. Pretty soon I seed there were a kind o' queer look on the water, an' I took a squint aloft at the sun. Bless you, boys, it looked queer!"

The Old Sailor paused, while the boys remained breathless with astonishment.

"I waked up the mate, and told him to look at it," continued the Old Sailor. "He jess rolled up one eye, said 'Jakes!' an' went fur to call the skipper. Nex' minute he was back on deck, a-yellin' fur all hands to shorten sail. The ole man came on deck, an' looked mighty ser'ous. He put all hands to work, and in an hour an' a half or so we had her down to close-reefed main-tops'l, storm-jib, an' spanker. All this time the sea were so smooth you couldn't see a ripple, an' we could hear the guinea-pigs a-squeakin' away down below, just as happy as if they was a-winnin' blue ribbons at San Seb. It were just noon w'en we got all made snug, an' at two bells a tramp steamer passed us. They hailed us, an' wanted to know why we didn't hoist a handkercher to help us along. The ole man says to 'em, says he: 'Shet up! You fellers 'll all be feedin' fish afore mornin'.' W'ich were gospel truth, 'cos they never was heerd tell of again. Howsumever, that ain't neither here nor there, seein' as how it 'ain't got nothin' to do with this 'ere yarn wot I'm a-tellin' you.

"Well, young gen'lemen, may I be keel-hauled if we didn't lie right in that werry identical spot till four o'clock in the afternoon before the storm wot were to have arrived arrove. An' then, my! my! It came down on to us as if it had been shot out of a gun. The sky turned so black in five minutes that it shone like patent-leather. Then, with a yell, the wind came down on us. There was a report like a cannon, an' our big main-tops'l were blowed right out o' the bolt-ropes. The old hooker heeled over till her lee rail were in the water, an' then she jumped forward like a skeert cat. But before she had gone a cable's-length, she came to a dead stop, an' stood straight up. The jib an' spanker was trimmed in flat; but I hope I'm a farmer if the jib didn't fill out to starboard an' the spanker to port. An' the blessed ole barky began to go round.

"'Down with your helm!' yelled the ole man.

"But, bless you! we didn't know w'ich were down, fur the wind were on our port beam forrard, an' on our starboard beam aft, an' wot were down for the jib were up for the spanker. We put the helm fust one way an' then the other, but it didn't make no difference. The *Central Park* jess kep' on goin' round an' round, faster an' faster, till she were spinnin' like a top.

"'Gee-menny!' yelled the ole man. 'We're right in the middle of a cyclone, an' we're a-revolvin' with it, an' we'll never get out o' this till the ole thing's blowed itself out!'

"'Cos, you know, a cyclone is a wind wot revolves. So round an' round the *Central Park* went, an' in half an hour every man jack aboard were as sick as a gal out yachtin'. By-an'-by the men began fur to lose their senses, an' in twenty-four hours all hands was ravin' lunatics exceptin' me. I started in to turn around the other way as fas' as I could, an' fur twenty-four hours I kep' sane. Then I got exhausted, an' staggered up ag'in' the mainmast, where, I guess, I kind o' fainted for a little while. When

I came to, I found that I were still the only sane man aboard, an' I wondered why. Then I seed that, leanin' ag'in' the mainmast, I were in the middle of the barky, where she went around so slow that it didn't have no effect on to me. Soon as I seed that, I called the other men there, an' in the course of the next few hours they all came to their senses. But the cyclone kep' right on. For ten days an' nights that ole hooker kep' goin' round like a pin-wheel on Fourth o' July. Then she begin to slow up. The clouds bruk away, an' the sun pecked out. The cyclone had blowed itself out.

"The ole man got out his pig-yoke an' shot the sun, an' found we'd been travellin' nearly sou'west till we was in the latitude o' the Magellans. You know where that is, of course. Waal, there was a sea runnin'. We shipped water by the acre. Somebody said that them there guinea-pigs must be all dead. I were sent below to look arter them. Bless you! w'en I got down there, they was all gone!

"Fur a minute I were kind o' dazed. Then I heard a squeakin' down below, an' I knowed the guinea-pigs was alive. I went down into the hold, an' there they all was. But the spectacles was all gone."

The boys looked at the Old Sailor in mute amazement. He continued:

"I didn't know what to think, but jess then one o' the guinea-pigs bit at my foot, an' I kicked him. Waal, boys, he rattled. Then I had a notion. I

picked up one o' them guineas, took him to the ole
man, an' told him wot I thought. He called the
cook, an' told him to kill the guinea. I hope I'm a
farmer if the critter weren't full o' spectacles. Durin'
them ten days an' nights no one had thought o' feedin' them pigs, an' they'd gnawed their way down into
the hold, an' filled up on spectacles. In three days
every guinea died from indigestion. So we put the
barky about, an' sailed back to Noo Yawk, havin'
been out four months, an' never gittin' anywhere
near our port o' destination. But, bless you! I hope
I'm a farmer if this ain't the sequel to this 'ere yarn
wot I've been a-tellin' you: Whenever I meets one
o' the men wot was shipmates with me aboard the
Central Park, he looks at me, an' I looks at him, an'
then we both falls to goin' around like a pair o' cock-
chafers, till we gits so full o' laugh that we can't
stand up."

The Old Sailor paused, and looked at the boys,
who were still transfixed with amazement.

"How do you like the wind, meanin' the yarn?"
asked the Old Sailor.

"Oh, very much, thank you!" answered the boys.

"Yes, an' it's putty good, too," said the Old
Sailor. And, turning his gaze once more upon the
distant horizon, he laughed another of his hearty,
quiet laughs.

It was a dull day, and the two boys did not know how to amuse themselves. All at once it occurred to Henry that they might go down and visit the Old Sailor.

"Perhaps," said the boy, "he will tell us another yarn."

"Please, sir, Mr. Old Sailor," said Henry, will you tell us another yarn?"

"What!" exclaimed the Old Sailor, "weren't the other one enough for you?"

"No, sir."

The Old Sailor gazed out over the water and laughed one of his silent laughs.

"S'pos'n'," he said, "I was to go fur to ask you wot kind o' a wessel were that one out yonder, wot 'd you say?"

"A light-ship!" answered both boys.

"Werry good, too," said the Old Sailor; "a light-ship are wot she be."

Then he indulged in another long, silent laugh, while both boys looked on in wonder.

"An' s'pos'n'," continued the Old Sailor, "I was

to go fur to ask you where she were bound, wot 'd you say ?"

" She isn't bound anywhere," answered Henry. " Light-ships stay in one place to mark the direction in which ships have to go to enter port."

Again the Old Sailor laughed and stared hard at a mere speck on the distant horizon.

" Oh, light - ships they stays in one place, does they?" he said. " Well, sometimes they does an' sometimes they doesn't. An' that's wot the yarn's about wot I'm a-goin' fur to tell you."

Both boys were now eagerly attentive. The Old Sailor took another look around the horizon, and, not seeing anything startling, fixed his gaze on the rolling red hull of the light-ship and began.

" This here yarn wot I'm a-goin' fur to tell you are about a yacht-race. You see, once upon a time, as they say in them there fairy tales wot kids ortn't to read ('cos sailor stories is better) — once upon a time I were sailin'-master o' the racin' schooner *Jabberwok* —"

" Could she galumph ?" asked Henry.

" Could she wot ?"

" Could she galumph ? You know the *Jabberwok* always went galumphing home."

" I don't know wot *Jabberwok* you're a-talkin' about, an' it are not perlite to interrupt gen'lemen wot's a-tellin' stories. This here schooner *Jabberwok* were a wall - sided old hooker an' a regular church for carryin' sail. Waal, it were in the spring regatta o' the Hog Island Yacht Club, an' there was four prizes up. The largest class were schooners 85 feet on the water-line an' over, an' the smallest were second-class sloops an' cutters 45 to 55 feet. You see, we didn't want no small fry in it, 'cos it were a extra ewent. The course were from a startin'-line off Buoy 15 in New York Bay to an' around the Sou'west Spit Buoy, thence to an' around the Sandy Hook Light-ship—that's where light-ships comes in—a-keepin' of the same on the starboard hand, an' back over the same course.

"Well," continued the Old Sailor, after pausing a moment to examine the horizon, "it were as beastly a mornin' as ever you see. I were down at Staten Island aboard the *Jabberwok*, a-waitin' for Mr. Parker, her owner. Mr. Parker were one o' the best amateur sailors wot ever gripped a king-spoke. He had passed his examination an' had a pilot's license, an' he was a good navigator, fit to navigate a ship around the world, that's wot he were. When he were aboard his own boat he were jest as good a sailin'-master as I were. Howsumever, as I were a-sayin', it were a dirty mornin'. The wind were no'theast an' freshenin', an' I made up my mind that we was a-goin' fur to have one o' the bloomingest, liveliest yacht-races wot ever got under way in them waters.

"Mr. Parker he came down on the judges' boat, the *E. W. Butter*, a mean an' contemptuable tug-boat. Mr. Parker says he to me, says he, 'It's goin' to be a big race,' an' I says to him, says I, it were.

With that I hove up the killick an' got the *Jabberwok*
under way. The startin'-gun were fired at 10:40,
and we had ten minutes fur to cross the line in. Of
course Mr. Parker sailed the *Jabberwok*, an' as usual
she were across the line fust, a-doin' it at 10:40:47.
The others followed along in this order: *Vamoose,
Skeerwagon, Pluffer, Ollagawalla, Tammany, Young
Duck, Edwin Booth, Veracious, Comet*, and *Get
There*. The *Get There* were always last. The *Jabberwok* crossed the line under fore an' mains'ls, workin' main-tops'l, jib, flyin' jib, and fore-staysail; an'
them sails was all a-pullin' like they was mad. The
Jabberwok tore through the water so fast that she
made it hot, an' steam rose behind her in her wake."

The boys stared at one another in open-mouthed
astonishment, while the Old Sailor gazed solemnly at
the light-ship. Then he continued:

"Well, it were jest about all that contemptuable
tug, the *E. W. Butter*, could do to keep within hailin'-distance o' the *Jabberwok* a-goin' down to the
Sou'west Spit. When we was off the inner end o'
the Swash Channel, the seas begin fur to come in
with a kind o' savagery that made me know we was
a-goin' for to have a damp time outside the Hook.
By-an'-by we rounded the Spit an' put her nose ag'in'
them seas. We was still a-leadin' the fleet about a
hundred yards, with the big cutter *Veracious* second, a-comin' after us like a scared dog. Well, as
soon as we headed up ag'in' them seas, I felt like
goin' back, fur our bowsprit began to climb up as if

it was a-goin' fur to jam a hole in the sky, an' then
it would come down again as if it was a-tryin' fur to
knock the plug out o' the bottom o' the Bay. Outside the big whitecaps was a-rollin', an' the surf
were a-poundin' on the Hook as though it were
a-tryin' fur to knock the p'int off. We weathered
the Hook all right, an' soon we was a-bilin' past
Buoy 5. The *Jabberwok* were a laborin'—maybe
that was wot you call galumphin'—an' so we took in
the main-tops'l an' housed both topmasts. When
that were done we was a little more comf'table, but
still it were not no bed o' daffadowndillies wot we
was a-reposin' on.

"By this time we was past the Scotland Light-
ship, an' were a-bearin' down on the Sandy Hook
Light-ship. The *Veracious* were on our weather
quarter, an' seemed to be a-gainin' on to us. The
judges' boat, the contemptuable tug, were away in
by the Hook. She didn't dare fur to come out, fur
no yacht-race had ever been sailed in such a sea, an'
the tug's cap'n were so skeert that he wanted to go
ashore. Well, boys, sich were the general sitiwa-
tion o' things, w'en, blow me fur a barnacle, if the
wind didn't die clean out, an' leave us a-jumpin'
around there helpless like a lot o' cork floats on a
fishin'-net. The yachts wot hadn't turned back—all
'cept we an' the *Veracious*—got up their topmasts
an' set club-tops'ls. There ain't much a yachtsman
won't do in a race, but that were a-haulin' it a leetle too taut.

"'Cos why.   You can't never tell wot's a-goin' fur to happen when a gale o' wind drops dead.   An' sure enough, all on a sudden, blow high an' blow out, out comes the wind out o' the nor'west a-screech-in' like four hundred cats with their tails stepped on. I heard one big crash, jest as if a house had caved in.   I looked back, an' every one o' them fellers wot had set club-tops'ls had carried away their topmasts. The last we saw o' them they was a-clearin' away the wreckage an' tryin' to beat back to the Hook.   Well, boys, in five minutes we had the most disruptious cross-sea on wot I ever knowed.   The *Jabberwok* seemed to sit right up on her taffrail sometimes, an' I told Mr. Parker I thought it wasn't no kind o' weather for a gen'leman to go to sea in.   But he said he'd never go back as long as that bloomin' cut-ter, the *Veracious*, stayed out; an' so we reefed close down fore an' aft, an' squared away fur Sandy Hook Light-ship, the *Veracious* followin' under bal-ance-reefed mains'l an' spitfire jib.

"An' now, boys," continued the Old Sailor, "comes the part o' this here yarn wot I'm a-tellin' you wot's goin' fur to astonidge you."

The boys looked at the Old Sailor eagerly as he went on thus :

"The more we sailed the more we didn't seem to get any nearer to that light-ship.   The hands for-rard got scared an' wanted to go back, but Mr. Par-ker wouldn't hear on't.   There were the *Veracious* a-hangin' on to our weather quarter, an' Mr. Parker were bound to go around that there light-ship ahead o' the fleet, or wot were left of it. But we couldn't get nowhere near the light-ship. Mr. Parker he says to me, says he, 'Heave the log.' An' I hove her, au' I reports to him, 'We're a-doin' of thirteen knots, sir,' says I to him, says I. Then we looked astern to see wot 'd become o' the other boats, an' bless you, we couldn't see nothin' at all of 'em. We couldn't see the Hook. We couldn't see the Highlands. Fact is, we was clean away out to sea with ten thousand screechin' furies of a gale a-blowin', an' a tumblin' stretch o' crazy sea ahead of us. Putty soon I made out that they wos a h'istin' some kind o' a flag aboard the light-ship. I got the glass on to it, an' made out it was the international code signal o' distress.

"'Salt mackerel an' buckwheat cakes!' says Mr. Parker; 'now I know wot's the matter.'

"'Wot d'you think?' says I.

"'The light-ship,' says he, 'has gone an' snapped her cables, an' she's runnin' away.'

"'Wot are you a-goin' fur to do?' says I.

"'I'm a-goin',' says he, 'to round that light-ship if I have to follow her to the Cape o' Good Hope.'

"'Well, sir,' says I, 'it won't take long at this gait.'

"Then I looks around, an' there were the *Veracious* still a-hangin' on to our weather quarter, an' bound to round the light-ship too. Blowin'? Well, boys, if a dog had tried to run ag'in' that wind it

'd 'a' blowed the ha'r right off his back. We was
a-scuddin' under bare poles, an' still a-goin' like a
express train. Well, I ain't a-goin' to tell you about
every day o' that trip, 'cos they was all alike. The
wind hauled more to the west'ard, an' we laid our
course dead afore it after the light-ship, wot couldn't
go no other way. So there was all three on us
— light-ship, *Jabberwok,* an' *Veracious* — whizzin'
straight across the ocean. One mornin' the lookout he sings out 'Land ho!' an' sure enough there
was the Rock o' Gibraltar right over our jib-boom.

"'Mr. Parker,' says I, 'it looks to me like that
there light-ship were a-goin' ashore.'

"'I'm a-goin' to round her,' says he, 'if she goes
up in the air.'

"He were a werry particular man, were Mr. Parker. Howsumever, there were the *Veracious* still
on our weather quarter, an' we wasn't goin' to be
beat by no sich craft. Well, shipwreck was a-starin'
of us all in the face when the gale broke, the wind
dropped to a moderate breeze, an' hauled to the
east'ard. An' then wot d' you s'pose happened?"

The boys signified that they were unable to suppose.

"Well," continued the Old Sailor, after one of his
silent laughs, "a tramp steamer comes out o' the
Mediterranean an' takes the light-ship in tow, an'
goes off towards America with her. Well, to say
that Mr. Parker were mad ain't tellin' you nothin'
at all. We fired guns an' made all kinds o' signals,

"'THERE WAS ONLY ONE THING TO DO, AND THAT WAS TO FOLLOW AS FAST AS WE COULD'"

but we couldn't get them there fellers to understand that we was sailin' a race an' wanted to round the light-ship. The tramp went right on, an', of course, as the wind were so light, we couldn't catch her. There were only one thing to do, an' that were to follow as fast as we could. An' there were the *Veracious* a-hangin' on to us just the same as before, only this time we was on her weather quarter. Well, boys, to get to the end o' this here yarn wot I'm a-tellin' you, we sailed back across the Atlantic, an' in due time we sights the Highland lights, an' begins to bear down on Sandy Hook once more. It were a fair to middlin' kind o' night, with a light wind an' an old sea on. Putty soon we sighted two red lights dead ahead. Mr. Parker squints at 'em through his glass, an' then he jumps fur the wheel.

"'There,' says he, 'are that bloomin' light-ship right back where she belongs, an' salt me down for a codfish if I don't round her now or carry away my head.'

"An' we rounded her, keepin' of her on the starboard hand, accordin' to the sailin' directions, the *Veracious*, wot had been with us all the time, roundin' at the same time an' a little behind us. Then we sailed up to the club's anchorage an' let go the mudhook. The next day Mr. Parker saw the Regatta Committee an' claimed the prize fur schooners, an' the owner o' the *Veracious* claimed the one fur sloops an' cutters, 'cos, don't you see, them was the only boats wot 'd rounded the light-ship."

2

The Old Sailor paused, and indulged in another long, silent laugh.

"And," said Henry, "did they get the prizes?"

"Not a bit of it," replied the Old Sailor. "The committee said they wasn't entitled to 'em 'cos they'd gone out o' their course. An' whose fault were that but the light-ship's, I'd like to know?"

Not long after the last yarn, on a very clear and calm day, when the sun was bright and the sea as smooth as oil, the boys became tired of play, and decided to go and talk to the Old Sailor, or, rather, let him talk to them. So they walked down to the pier, and there, as usual, sat their friend gazing out to sea. The boys often wondered what it was that the Old Sailor was looking for out there, but as he never told them, they never found out. Away out on the horizon were two three-masted schooners with every stitch of canvas spread to catch the faint upper current of air that hardly gave them steerageway. Off to the southward a little squat lead-colored fruit steamer, with a gaudy red-topped funnel, was rolling lazily along on the last stretch of her voyage from Havana, her lumbering sway resembling for all the world the motion of a duck walking. Off in the northeast four short masts and two columns of smoke rose far enough above the blue rim of the sea to let the spectator know that an ocean greyhound was slipping along. Half-way between these and the two schooners, but much nearer to the land, was a curious old-fashioned brig, with a very high poop, a top-gallant forecastle, single topsails, and a bowsprit that stood up in front of her almost like a mast. The Old Sailor turned his head slightly when he heard the footsteps of the boys behind him.

"There she blows!" said the Old Sailor.

"Who?" asked Henry.

"You, in course," replied their friend. "That's wot we says aboard o' a whalin'-wessel when we sees a whale."

"Were you ever a sailor on a whaling-ship?"

"S'posin' I wos to ax you wot kind o' a wessel were that," said the Old Sailor, pointing at the old-fashioned brig, "wot 'd you go fur to say?"

"A brig," exclaimed both boys.

"W'y?"

"Because she has two masts, both square-rigged."

"Werry good, too, says I. An' s'posin' I wos to ax you wot kind o' trade she were in, wot 'd you say?"

"I don't know," said Henry.

"That's werry good, too. W'en you don't know nothin', say so an' stick to it. Mebbe you might learn."

Then the Old Sailor stared out at the sea and laughed a long, silent laugh. "Now I'm a-goin' fur to tell you a secret," he continued, presently. "I don't know neither."

He laughed again, and the boys laughed too.

"But," said the Old Sailor, "she looks like a old

whalin'-brig called the *Merry Grampus* wot I were oncet first mate on, which the same time I went into some werry high latitudes, an' come putty near not comin' back never no more."

"Oh, tell us about that!" exclaimed both boys, knowing that their quaint friend had another yarn ready for them.

"This 'ere yarn wot I'm a-goin' fur to tell you," began the Old Sailor, watching the brig and shaking his head gravely, "are a werry curious yarn, an' it all happened in the summer o' 1848. The brig *Merry Grampus* were commanded by Cap'n Jehosaphat Snodgrass, a werry tall, thin man wot did most o' his talkin' through his nose, though I didn't see no need o' that, 'cos his mouth were as big as a moorin' pipe, an' his ears wos too. Howsumever, that 'ain't got nothin' to do with the yarn wot I'm a-goin' fur to tell you. Cap'n Jehosaphat Snodgrass were mortal fond o' carryin' sail, an' he never were so happy as when he had all his stuns'ls on. So it were not so werry many days afore we wos at the entrance to Davis's Straits, which is the front door o' the north pole. We had been doin' putty well, an' had some considerable number o' barrels o' oil stowed away below; but now luck fell dead agin us, an' it seemed as ef every whale had gone South to spend the summer in warm latitudes, which wos contrary to nature.

"To make things wuss an' wuss, it came on to blow from the north'ard an' west'ard, an' Cap'n

Jehosaphat Snodgrass he ups an' he says, says he, 'I'll be blowed ef I'm a-goin' to butt agin a gale like a bloomin' Flyin' Dutchman,' says he just like that to me, as wos first mate. 'Werry well, sir,' says I; 'ef you don't heave to, you got to scud,' says I to him, says I. 'Then let her scud,' says he to me, says he, just like that. So I got the old hooker under a close-reefed main-tops'l an' double-reefed fores'l, an' I let her go south-s'utheast. We ran that way fur about ten hours, an' then the sea begin to git too high fur us to run any more; so the Cap'n he says, says he, that we'd have to heave to, arter all, an' wuss luck to it. So we hove her to on the port tack. But, bless you! we hadn't much more'n got it done, when, bizz! the wind smacks around to the sou'west an' blows the sea out flat-ter 'n a New England slapjack. Then Cap'n Jehosaphat Snodgrass says he to me, says he, 'We got to heave her to this new wind on the starboard tack, 'cos ef we go on the port tack we'll fetch up on Cape Farewell, which the same it are a werry im-proper place fur to fetch up on, me knowin', 'cos I bin there.' An' says I to him, says I, 'Werry well, sir; I don't want to fetch up on Cape Fare-well, nor no other cape, 'cos dry land ain't no place fur the keel o' a ship.' So we heaves her to on the starboard tack, an' there we stayed fur three days an' nights. All the time we wos makin' about seven p'ints leeway, an' w'en the gale broke the Cap'n he figured it out that we wos not fur to the south'ard an' east'ard o' Cape Discord, which, as you werry well knows, is on the east coast."

"East coast of what?" asked Henry.

"East coast o' Greenland, o' course," answered the Old Sailor. "You didn't suppose that w'en we wos in Davis's Straits we wos off the Cape o' Good Hope, did you?"

The boys looked abashed, and the Old Sailor, after indulging in one of his silent laughs, proceeded thus:

"Waal, arter the gale ended, the lookout was stationed in the crow's-nest agin, an' we hoped we might see a whale putty soon. We hadn't much faith, howsumever, 'cos we'd never done no whalin' on that side o' Greenland, an' didn't know much about it; neither did nobody else, so fur as I know. Howsumever, it weren't so werry long before, while we wos a standin' to the sou'west under heavy canvas, the lookout sings out, 'There she blows, an' there she breaches!'

"'W'ere away?' says I to him, says I.

"'Two p'ints off the lee bow!' says he to me, says he.

"Waal, Cap'n Jehosaphat Snodgrass he comes on deck in about two jumps, an' orders me to take the second boat, an' he wos goin' to take the fust himself. We lowered away, an' wos just a-startin' from the ship's side, w'en the lookout sings out agin, an' we learned that there was another whale up an' blowin' about half a mile away from the fust.

The Cap'n started with his boat arter this new one, an' I went arter the one wot 'd bin sighted fust. Waal, I sees when we begin to bear down on him that he were a werry big an' powerful-lookin' bull whale, an' I got ready to have a lively scrimmage. I handled the harpoon myself, an' I sent it in, as I thought, putty deep. The whale up flukes an' sounds, an' the line run out o' the tub like lightnin' fur a minute or two, I tell you. He didn't go werry deep, though, an' soon he come up, shootin' half his length out o' the water. Then he started off fur the north pole as hard as he could tear. Gee-whizz! —the way we went through the water fur a minute or two! Then I looked down at the line, an' I wos scared to see that it were frayed, an' ready to break. I grabbed it outside the boat's gunnel. Jest then the whale gives a jump, bang went the line, an' I were overboard an' goin' through the water like a express train."

The boys almost held their breath in anxiety.

"W'en I come to the surface," continued the Old Sailor, "I were a hundred an' fifty yards from the boat, still hangin' on to the line, an' bein' towed through the sea about twelve knots an hour. I were such a poor swimmer I knowed I couldn't git back to the boat, an' I knowed no boat could catch me a-goin' at that gait. I made up my mind my time had come, but I says to myself, says I, 'I won't go under till I've got to.' So I turned over on my back an' hung on. As long as the whale kept a-goin' I couldn't sink. He kept on fur I don't know how long—two or three hours—an' I were putty near dead. The brig an' boats wos out o' sight long ago. Then all on a sudden the whale he stopped an' turned back, comin' right at me. Then I gave up an' let go the line. Of course I went down, an' when I came up I came up right alongside o' the whale, wot were lyin' puffickly still. 'Dead,' I thought, believin' I'd sent the harpoon in fur enough to bleed him to death. But I were sinkin' agin. I grabbed out with both hands, an' by good-luck caught the harpoon line. I hauled myself up to the surface an' got my breath. 'Ef the whale's dead,' says I to myself, says I, 'he'll float.' So by means o' the line I climbs up on his back. Waal, I weren't so werry much better off than I were before, 'cos floatin' around on a dead whale in the North Atlantic ain't such sport as it might seem to them wot hasn't tried it.

"Waal, I puzzled my brains as to wot I were to do next. Generally speaking, I knowed the land were somewhere to the west'ard o' me, an' it couldn't be so werry fur away neither, owin' to the distance the whale had towed me towards it. How were I to get there? The wind were now a fair breeze from the east'ard, an' I says to myself, says I, 'Ef I could only rig a sail on this 'ere whale, an' steer him somehow, mebbe I could sail myself ashore.' Waal, there wos the harpoon an' and the line—one spar an' plenty o' riggin'. But ef I used the harpoon fur

a mast it weren't tall enough, an' I wouldn't have
no yard. So I were putty much puzzled. But
byme-by I jumps up with a new idee. 'Wot's the
reason I can't make a mast out o' myself?' says I
to myself, says I, just like that. So I takes off my
shirt, an' with my knife an' yarns from the harpoon
line I soon had a werry good sail made. Then I
had an awful time a-pullin' the harpoon out o' the
whale. Out she came, though, an' not a speck o'
blood followed, w'ich struck me all in a heap,
till I remembered that he wouldn't bleed arter he
were dead. I bent my sail on to the harpoon, an'
then I made a parral 'round my neck, by means
o' which I slung my yard. I made the sheets
fast to my feet, an' I were ready to get under
way."

"But how did you steer?" said Henry.

"W'y, I just rigged lines on to his tail, an' w'en
I wanted to steer, pulled his tail fur a rudder.

"Waal, I carc'lated I were makin' about two
knots an hour," continued the Old Sailor, "an' I
were considerable worried about the wind holdin',
or whether I'd git ashore afore I starved to death.
Howsumever, to make the story short, I sailed all
night, and as soon as daylight come I sees land dead
ahead, about four miles away. Now I wished I
knowed how much water that whale drawed, so's I
could tell what kind o' a harbor to make fur. I
looked mighty close at the land which I were approachin', but I couldn't see no inlet. But putty

"'THE WHALE GIVE A GREAT BIG SHIVER, SENT ME A-FLYIN' INTO THE AIR, AN' DISAPPEARED'"

soon I did see somethin' wot pleased me a heap more, an' that were an Esquimau a-comin' off in his dak. He'd seed me a-comin', an' wos bound to find out wot kind o' a craft I were. He pulled up about fifty yards away, an' axed me wot I were. I told him as quick as I could, an' says to him, says I, to please take me off.

"Waal, young gen'lemen, before he could make a stroke, I felt a sudden earthquake under me. The whale give a great big shiver, humped his back, threw up his flukes, sent me a-flyin' into the air, an' disappeared. Luckily fur me, I'd already taken off my harpoon yard, so, arter sinkin' putty deep, I came up agin, an' the Esquimau, who had made a good guess, were right there an' grabbed me. He pulled me into his boat, where I sat puffickly dumb fur a few minutes. W'en I looked up the Esquimau were a-laffin' at me. 'Putty good joke, I s'pose,' says I, 'but I don't see it.' 'Why,' says he, 'you ort to be satisfied. That whale saved your life.' I says to him, says I, 'That's all werry well, but that whale were dead, an' hadn't no business to come to life agin like that.'

"'Dead? Nonsense!' says the Esquimau, paddlin' me towards the land. 'He were asleep.'

"'Asleep?' says I; 'with a harpoon in him?'

"'Yes,' says he to me, says he, laffin' still more; 'you hit him on the funny-bone with it w'en you struck him, an' jest put him to sleep arter the first shock were over. It always does. We Esquimaux often harpoon whales on the funny-bone just fur the fun o' the thing.'"

The Old Sailor looked gravely around the horizon for a moment, and then concluded thus:

"I got home agin all right in the course o' time, or I wouldn't be here; but I 'ain't never believed that that Esquimau told the truth."

ONCE again the Old Sailor was sitting on the end of the pier, gazing out to sea according to his custom. The two boys were approaching him, burning with a desire to hear one more of his wonderful stories. He was unaware of their approach, and was lost in contemplation of the beautiful scene spread out before him. There was a good wholesail breeze from the south, and vessels bound in were making the water fly around their bows in clouds of smokelike spray. High, wall-sided, three-masted schooners were marching along wing-and-wing, looking as proud and stiff as militia colonels on review, while a little farther out a magnificent four-masted ship, with double tops and skysails, was gliding on with the easy dignity of an old major-general of regulars watching the volunteers. The vessels bound to the southward, on the other hand, were all on a taut bow-line, some on the port and some on the starboard tack, but all heeled far over, and fussing through the choppy seas at a great pace. Far out on the sharply outlined horizon a four-masted Havana steamer was cutting her way through the foaming ridges at a good fourteen-knot gait. Half-way between her and the shore was the most interesting sight of all—the North Atlantic squadron of the navy, or a part of it, moving majestically along at ten knots an hour towards New York. The *Philadelphia*, rolling uneasily as is her wont, was at the head of the fleet, flying the Admiral's flag; the stanch and threatening *Atlanta* followed; then came the picturesque monitor *Miantonomoh;* and last of all the trim dynamite cruiser *Vesuvius.* It was upon this handsome fleet that the Old Sailor's gaze was fastened when the boys went up and bade him good-morning.

"Good-mornin' to you, my lads," he said. "An' wot might you s'pose that to be?" He pointed at the sailing ship.

" A four-masted ship," answered both boys.

" An' w'en a ship has four masts instead o' three, w'ich is accordin' to nature, wot d' ye call the last mast o' the four?"

" Jigger."

"Werry good, too. An' wot d' ye call that out yonder?" He pointed to the steamer.

" Why," said Henry, " that's a steamer, of course."

"Of course, says you. But where d' ye s'pose she might be bound?"

" Charleston?"

"Savannah?"

"Not so werry good," said the Old Sailor, after indulging in one of his quiet laughs. " That's guessin', an' guessin' ain't knowin'. That steamer are bound fur Havana, an' she ain't bound fur nowhere else."

"But how can you tell that?" asked Henry.

"I knows it by her build. She's a Morgan liner, an' that means she are bound fur Havana. But I 'ain't said nothin' yet about the most important wessels wot is under our observation." So saying, the Old Sailor gravely turned his back on the boys, who gazed wonderingly over the animated waters.

"Oh, I see!" exclaimed Henry. "They are warships."

"Werry good, too, says you," said the Old Sailor, bestowing a glance of approval on his young friend. "Them is war-ships. How might you know that?"

"I can tell them from the pictures I've seen in HARPER'S WEEKLY," said Henry.

"W'ich goes fur to show that picture papers is some good. Now, could you tell the names o' them ships?"

"I know one," answered Henry. "The little flat one with two turrets and one short mast is the *Miantonomoh*."

"Werry good, too, says you. An' the other ones is the *Philadelphia*, the *Atlanta*, an' the *Vesuvius*. Them 'ere wessels has set me a-thinkin' about old times, because they's so different from the sort of wessels wot we had in the war."

"Were you ever a sailor on a war-ship?"

"My son, I were. There ain't no kind o' hooker

trayversin' the great deep wot I 'ain't served on somehow an' somewhere."

"Did you ever fire a cannon?"

"Yes, an' also the cannoneer. An' I've been in fights, too; but none o' 'em warn't nothin' alongside o' the fun we had with blockade-runners."

"What are they?"

"Waal, you see it's like this. A seaport town depends putty largely on wessels fur its supplies. Now durin' the war a fleet o' United States wessels would lie off the harbor o' a Confederate town, an' stop every craft wot tried to git in or out. The blockade-runners wos fast steamers wot made it their business to slip through the fleet an' git in with supplies. D' ye see?"

"Yes," answered Henry. "It must have been mighty dangerous work."

"Waal, generally it were. 'Cos w'y, no matter how keerful they might be about paintin' their ships lead-color an' runnin' in on thick nights, sometimes we wos bound to see 'em, an' then the way we'd let loose on to 'em with our great guns wos a sight fur blind mice. I tell you they must 'a' been mighty plucky fellers to run in through sich fire as we give 'em sometimes; but they done it, they did—that is, they all done it 'ceptin' one, an' he run the blockade by stayin' outside."

"Oh, how was that?" asked Henry.

"Waal, the incidents o' this 'ere yarn wot I'm a-goin' fur to tell you took place in the summer o'

1863, w'en a blockadin' fleet o' no less 'n thirty Union wessels wos a-lyin' at anchor outside o' Charleston. I war a-sarvin' aboard the *George Washington*, which the same she war a old-fashioned, brig-rigged side-wheeler, an' carried six eight-inch Dahlgren guns. We wos a-layin' on the outside o' the whole fleet, 'cos we wos considered werry fast, an' it were our business fur to chase any wessel wot got past the rest o' the fleet comin' out. One afternoon I war on lookout at the mast-head an' I sees a light thin smoke away down on the southern horizon. So I sings out, 'Steamer ho!' An' the ossifer o' the deck says he to me, says he, 'W'ere away?' 'Three points off the port bow,' says I to him, says I, just like that. 'Keep your eye on her,' says he. An' that's wot I war a-doin' of all the time; but I didn't say nothin' 'ceptin', 'Aye, aye, sir,' 'cos it aren't considered perlite to say werry much to the ossifer o' the deck. This 'ere steamer she come right along, an' soon I made her out to be a fast side-wheeler, but she weren't painted no lead-color. The ossifer o' the deck called the cap'n, an' he ordered the crew to quarters."

"What is that?" asked Henry.

"W'en you go to quarters, you get everything ready fur to fight," continued the Old Sailor. "But, bless me, if this 'ere steamer didn't stop just out o' range an' lay a-rollin' on the swell. Then we got a signal from the commandin' ossifer o' our squadron to chase her. You see there warn't no doubt now

3

but she war a blockade-runner, but we couldn't see wot she meant by runnin' right up to us in daytime. Waal, we hove up the anchor an' started, but, bless you! she just run away from us. But that warn't the wust on't. W'en we turned around to come back, so did she, keepin' out o' range all the time. We turned around an' chased her again, but as soon as we started back so did she. Waal, would you believe it, we kept that up till dark; an' then there she war a-lyin' just out o' range o' the whole fleet."

The Old Sailor looked around the horizon, indulged in a quiet laugh, and went on thus:

" By order o' the squadron commander all lookouts were doubled, an' we stood by to give that there wessel rats if she tried to run in. But w'en the day broke there she wos a-lyin' in the same spot. We got up the *George Washington's* anchor an' gave chase. Bless you, it war the same business all over again. She'd run away, an' come back w'en we did; an' at nightfall the next night there she war still. The next night war a clear moonlight one, an' we knowed she couldn't get in. Still we watched close. About two bells in the fust watch, w'ich the same that is 9 P.M., I seed a queer-lookin' craft comin' out. It war low and flat, an' didn't have no masts nor no smoke-stack. All the same it wos a-goin' along at a ten-knot gait. I tell you wot, boys, it give us sailor-men the shivers, fur it looked edzackly like a ghost of a wrecked ship; an' that's wot we thought it war. 'No good o' firin' at that thing,' said Pete Martin;

'our shots 'd go through them sides an' never hit nothin' at all.' All the same, the cap'n give orders to let her have it, and we opened fire."

"Did you hit her?"

"Hit your grandmother's sneeze!" exclaimed the Old Sailor. "No, we didn't hit her. Pete Martin vowed he saw one ball go straight through her, and it looked like a ball goin' through a cloud o' smoke. She went right on an' fetched up alongside o' the curious steamer. There she stayed all night, an' we could see 'em lowerin' away stuff off the steamer into this 'ere canal-boat-lookin' craft. The cap'n said we'd sink her sure as she tried to run in. Towards mornin' she started at the liveliest kind o' a gait. Every one o' our wessels in range o' her opened up, an' there war noise enough to scare a boiler-maker. One shot struck the water about a cable's length ahead o' the queer craft. Then there rose up a big boilin' cloud o' spray right w'ere the shot struck, an' the next thing we knowed that 'ere craft jumped forward at a seventeen-knot gait, an' jist fairly flew into the harbor. Pete Martin says he to me, says he, 'They've got old Davy Jones hitched to her with a tow-rope and he's a-pullin' o' her.' An' blow me fur pickles ef it didn't look as ef Pete war right!

"The next mornin'," continued the Old Sailor, "the strange steamer went away, but in a week she came back, an' the same fun begins all over again. On the second day, while we wos a-watchin' the

strange steamer, we seed a whale. It wos a curious
thing that a whale should be around there, an' Pete
Martin says he to me, says he, 'That whale smells
a thrasher.'"

"What is that?" asked Henry.

"It are a kind o' shark," answered the Old Sailor,
"wot fights by thrashin' with his tail. I didn't say
nothin', but jest kep' a-watchin'. That night we wos
ordered to man the boats an' try to board the ghost-
boat w'en it war returnin' from the strange steamer.
Sure enough, it came out, rushin' along in the same
old spooky sort of a way, without no noise an' no
sign o' steam or sail. There come putty nigh bein'
a mutiny among the crew o' the *George Washington*,
'cos we didn't want to board no sich wessel; but the
ossifers was detarmined, an' so we stood by. While
we wos a-waitin' I heerd the whale blow, an', sure
enough, there he war, not more 'n fifty yards away
from us, lyin' quiet on the sea. Putty soon the
ghost-boat started fur home, an' we got our cutlasses
an' rewolwers ready fur business. An' now comes
the funny part."

The Old Sailor paused a moment while the boys
waited anxiously to hear the rest of his yarn.

"Jess as the ghost-boat war bearin' down on us,"
he continued, "I seed that whale give himself a
shake an' go down. Then all on a suddent, about a
cable's length ahead o' the ghost-boat, there began
the liveliest sort o' a scrimmage. The sea boiled an'
the whale come a-shootin' out half his length. The

next second another fish shot into the air an' come
down on the water with the report o' a cannon.
Flop, flop, bang, swash, swizzle! My, my! You
never seed such a row! An' the ghost-boat come to
a dead stop! Bang, bang! went the whale an' the
other fish fur about five minutes! 'Give way!' yells
the ossifers. But bless you, not a sailor-man could
move. We wos all flabbergasted. Waal, the rumpus
came to an end, an' wot do you think we seed?"

"What?"

"That there whale was deader 'n a door-nail, an'
right alongside o' him war layin' a thrasher, w'ich
the same war deader than another door-nail. 'By
the great horn spoon!' says Pete Martin, just like
that, 'they had that thrasher towin' that ghost-boat,
an' it ain't no ghost-boat at all.' An' in less 'n two
minutes we wos aboard the queer craft, an' she war
ours. Her cap'n war a-sittin' flat on the deck a-cryin'
as if his heart 'd break. 'Oh dear, oh dear!' says
he, 'my thrasher is dead! my thrasher is dead! An'
I loved him like he war my own child, w'ich the
same he war, seein' that I brought him up myself
from the egg, an' taught him to fetch an' carry, an'
to tow boats, an' to run the blockade. An' now he's
gone, an' I sha'n't never be able to swindle the Yan-
kees no more. Oh dear, oh dear, oh dear!'

"An' that," said the Old Sailor, rising, with a very
grave face, "are the end o' this yarn wot I'm a-tellin'
you, an' also of the thrasher wot run the blockade
an' met a whale wot war out o' his latitood."

A REAL AFRICAN SWELL

THE Old Sailor was in a state of excitement. He did not wait for the boys to go down to his humble dwelling and endeavor to persuade him to tell them one of his surprising yarns. He ran up to their house instead, and, bursting in with a rush, exclaimed:

"Mebbe you will and mebbe you won't; 'tain't fur me fur to go fur to say. But ef you don't, you is chumpish."

"What ever do you mean?" cried Henry.

"Cap'n Gawge Hennery Bagg, wot were skipper o' the brig *Ellen Mush* w'en I war fust mate o' her, an' wot got wracked on the east coast o' Afrikee, are come to wisit me, an' ef you don't come down an' hear wot he's got to say, you'll be mighty sorry."

The boys sprang up and at once followed the Old Sailor, who led the way to the village hotel. Perhaps his statement that Captain Bagg had come there expressly to visit him was a slight exaggeration. At any rate, the captain had just returned from a long visit at the summer home of a wealthy steamship owner near the pier.

"Cap'n Bagg," said the Old Sailor, "here is them

two young gen'lemen wot I war a-tellin' ye about, wot has so much fondness fur hearin' about my adwentures on the briny deep."

Captain Bagg shook hands with the boys, and said,

"And I suppose they would like to hear a story from me."

"Yes!" cried both boys.

"Well," said the captain, "it was this way: This Old Sailor was my first mate on the brig *Ellen Mudge*—"

"*Mush*, I allus called her," said the Old Sailor.

"And," continued the captain, "we were bound from New York to Mozambique. We had a beautiful run of it down to the Cape of Good Hope. I dare say I counted my chickens before they were hatched, for we had not fairly begun to make northing before it piped up from the south-southeast, and the weather speedily grew worse and worse till it was blowing a real gale. I hove her to on the starboard tack, and soon the wind hauled more to the eastward and blew harder than ever. Two days and nights we were hove to, and neither I nor your old friend there had any rest. On the afternoon of the third day a hand forward sung out, 'Land ho!' There it was, sure enough, dead under our lee, and a raging, howling sea breaking on the rocks. To make a long story short, at five o'clock I let go both bowers in seventeen fathoms. We dragged, and I ordered the masts cut away. We stopped dragging, but in a short time our terrible pitching snapped one cable, and the other could not hold her ; so in we went, crashing broadside on against the rocks.

"I will not pain you by telling you how my men were swept overboard. All I need to say is that your old friend and I were carried off the poop deck by a monster sea, and that was all I knew till I found myself clinging to a huge rock. I climbed up and reached a sheltered niche in the side of the cliff, where I remained all night. In the morning I searched for my men, but found not a trace of any one save our old friend here, who had also reached a high part of the rocks. Our comrades were all drowned, and the brig was broken in three pieces. So we climbed to the top of the cliff, and saw a fine level piece of country running back from the sea. Behind a clump of trees about a mile away rose some smoke."

"An' I says to you, says I," exclaimed the Old Sailor, "there are a camp o' savages, an' we'll probably be fried, broiled, or fricasseed fur breakfast."

"You did," continued Captain Bagg ; "and I answered that I was too hungry to care much who ate so long as there was some eating going on. Well, we crept through the high grass till we were near enough to see through the bushes. And what do you think we saw?"

"Twenty fierce cannibals in war paint grouped around a fire eating their horrid meal !" exclaimed Henry.

"Not at all," said the captain, smiling. "We saw a very neat garden, full of rose-bushes, surrounding a very pretty white house. It looked for all the world like a modest country residence in England. While we were wondering what sort of people could live in such a house away out in the wilds of east Africa, a man appeared in the garden. He had on a straw hat and a white flannel suit, and was smoking a cigarette. His hat was pulled down so low in front that we could not see his face, but his dress and his manner assured us that he was an Englishman. So we stepped out and advanced boldly. I said, 'Good-morning, sir,' and he looked up. And what do you suppose?"

"What?" exclaimed the boys.

"He was a genuine African, as black as the coal in your father's cellar. He took the cigarette out of his mouth, put a single eye-glass in his left eye, and, after blowing a cloud of smoke, said, 'When did you come up?' 'Up where?' I asked. 'Up the river, of course.' 'What river?' said I. 'Why, the Nile,' said he. 'You all come up the Nile, don't you?' 'I did not come up the Nile,' I replied. 'I came from the sea.' 'Really,' he said; 'but it doesn't make a bit of difference; here you are. But I really don't see that you can do anything. It's all been done to death, ye know, my dear boy, quite too dreadfully done to death, really.' 'What do you mean?' I asked him. 'Can it be possible that you don't know where you are?' 'Not exactly,' I said. 'I'm some-

where on the east coast of Africa, but I lost my
reckoning before I arrived.' 'Then,' he replied, 'per-
mit me to enlighten you. You are in darkest Africa, and I am King Ubinam, of whom you have doubt-
less read accounts by several explorers. I really can't
see why you have come to go over the old ground
again. It's all been written up by Stanley and those
other fellows, though I regret to say that their accounts are very faulty. I am preparing a volume
for publication myself. It is to be given out first in
the form of letters, which will be printed simultane-
ously in England and America, and afterwards col-
lected in book form. Each letter will contain six
illustrations, reproduced from kodak photographs
taken by myself, and signed with a fac-simile of
my autograph. I get one pound extra per letter
for the use of the autograph. So you see, my dear
fellow, you are quite out of it, and you'd better
go back, 'pon my honor.' 'But,' I said, 'we are
no explorers. We are shipwrecked mariners. Seeing the smoke from your chimney, we thought
there might be a camp of savages, or even cannibals, and we might get a bite to eat.' The king
laughed. 'Savages! Cannibals!' he said. 'Why,
my dear fellow, you're quite behind the times. We
don't have those things any more. We've been ex-
plored, and we've learned the habits of our European
discoverers. But come into the palace and breakfast with me, and you shall meet my daughters.
They'll give you a royal welcome when they learn

that you are not explorers. We so seldom see any one here except explorers, for it *is* a little off the lines of travel.'"

Here the Old Sailor, slapping his hand on his knee, broke in. "Waal, boys, you never seed no sich gals as them there two wot I'm a-tellin' you of. One on 'em were about six feet high, an' had sich ears an' han's an' feet as I never seed off a monkey. T'other one were short an' fat an' yaller, like thin maple syrup. The tall one were called Gladys, an' the short one Gwendoline. An' their mammar were both short an' thin, an' were called Her Majesty, but her real name were Maria. For dinner they had some roast beef—roast beef o' old England were wot the king called it. I think it were roasted in a tin wash-boiler full o' water; leastways that were how it tasted. But beggin' your pardon, cap'n; this 'ere's your yarn, so heave ahead."

"The king said to me," continued the captain, "'We always have our beef cooked this way. You see, the truth of the matter is, dear boy, that we've quite fallen into English habits.' And then Gwendoline turned to our old friend here and said, 'Awfully jolly, don't you think?' And he said he hadn't met with anything so jolly since he'd been half tickled to death by a porcupine which had crawled into his bunk on the coast of Morocco. I tried to warn him not to talk that way, and I heard Gwendoline whisper to him: 'You're chaffing us; you know you are. But we are up to chaff, really. But, for

goodness' sake, be careful that you don't irritate
papa. When he's aroused, he's very terrible, 'pon
honah !' "

" Waal, I tried to be decent to him," broke in the
Old Sailor, " 'cos he were a king, an' wore a white
flannel suit ; but, by the great horn spoon, the plum-
puddin' were too bloomin' much fur me. So I says
to him : 'Kingsy, if any explorer told you that this
'ere were plum-puddin', he were a-givin' you a bilin'
twister. It's duff, that's wot it are—duff, an' blame
poor duff, too.' Waal, that poor king he looked
down into his plate, an' he hove a sigh like a grampus, an' then he looks at me from under his eyebrows most sorrowful - like, and says he : 'Deary
me ! Deary me !' But beggin' your pardon, cap'n ;
perceed."

" Her majesty," continued the captain, " put her
napkin up to her eyes, and burst into tears. 'If you
talk that way, Ubinam,' she sobbed, 'I'll never get
into society, never ;' and the gals both looked very
sad. So our old friend said, 'It ain't so werry bad,
an' I'll take a little more.' And then the king
looked more melancholy than ever, and rose from
the table, saying, 'I hate a man who tells the truth
and then tries to fib out of it.' With that he lit a
cigarette, and went out into the garden. The two
girls took us into the library, and explained to us
that the queen had to do her own cooking, because
they couldn't hire servants in that part of the world,
and they feared that she would worry herself into a

decline if she didn't soon conquer the mysteries of
those British dishes, because his majesty would tol-
erate nothing that was not English. 'But,' I said,
'if she keeps on this way, the king will die of dys-
pepsia.' Gladys looked at Gwendoline, and said:
'Maybe that is what is troubling papa now. Oh, if
we could only get him to eat men again as he used
to do in the good old days before the explorers came
and made us so very English!' And both the girls
looked at us so very earnestly that I said, with much
emphasis: 'Oh, I'd wait awhile if I were you, and
give your mother a fair chance. She hasn't got the
hang of it yet.' 'No,' said Gladys; 'that's it; and
she *does* cook a man so beautifully!'

"Well, boys, we did not sleep very soundly that
night, for we were afraid they might take a sudden
notion to have us for breakfast. But we hadn't
counted on the firmness with which the English
ideas had hold of the king. We forced some of the
dreadfully cooked food down our throats the next
day, but it was hard. The king watched us all the
time. We ate less and less as the days went by,
and the king grew more and more solemn, and
didn't eat much himself. Things went on this way,
and we found no opportunity to escape, till one day,
about three weeks after our wreck, the king sprang
up from the dinner-table, having eaten nothing, and
cried out, 'Fijont, sitilisnot, feeb dna egabbac!'
Her majesty turned a little pale, looked frightened,
but sprang up and cried out, 'Ti fo kniht tnod!'

The king said, 'Lliw I!' And the two girls clapped
their hands in delight and screamed, 'Ap rof sreehc
eerht!' We were alarmed, for we did not know
what it all meant. The next thing we knew all four
of them dashed out of the dining-room and ran up-
stairs. Our old friend here said, 'Cap, I reckon
we'd better stand by to slip cables.' He was right.
We went out into the garden, and had hardly done
so when we heard yells, and out came the whole
family on the run, the king leading. He had taken
off his English clothing. He wore a string of feath-
ers around his waist, a ring in his nose, and a silk
hat on the back of his head. In his hand he carried
a huge knife. The girls and the queen, also in savage dress, followed, the queen bringing up the rear
with a big iron kettle on her arm. We did not
stop."

"We cut cables, an' set stuns'ls," said the Old
Sailor. "We got under way all standin', as ye
mought say, an' steered fur the open sea. We
grabbed up our life presarvers from the place we'd
hid 'em, put 'em on as we run, an' jumped into the
sea. We struck out fur the offin', fur we didn't
know but that there Anglified old cannibal might
sprout a canoe as quick as he had a knife. But it
seems he didn't have one. We swum out, an' out,
an' out, till we got tired, an' then we floated. You
know we didn't get drownded—'cos w'y? we're
here. W'ich the same it are, 'cos we wos picked up
the next mornin' by a steam-yacht wot wos makin' a

v'yage round the world, an' we worked our way home in her. But beggin' your pardon, cap'n, this here are your yarn."

"Well," said the captain, "anyhow you've finished it."

THE ocean was shrouded behind an impenetrable curtain of gray, for it was a morning of dense, chilling fog. Nevertheless the Old Sailor sat on the end of the pier and gazed seaward. The boys, who were wandering about disconsolately in the vain hope of finding something to amuse them, were surprised and delighted when they found him there.

"This is just the kind of a day for a yarn," said Henry.

"Oh yes," said George, "and perhaps it will be all about a fog."

So they sat down beside the Old Sailor. He did not seem to see them. He continued to gaze steadily into the fog, and to mutter indistinctly. The boys gazed into the fog, too. They could see dull brown lines forming and advancing and spreading until they rolled out of the fog as slow, shiny breakers, toppling over and bursting into dingy, leaden spray right under the pier. The very sound of the surf seemed choked. They could hear every minute the long, hoarse blast of a steamer's whistle, warning other craft that she was approaching. Between the blasts of the steamer's whistle they could hear the tooting of a strident fog-horn aboard some sailing-vessel, and occasionally the ringing of the fog-bell on the light-ship would come faintly across the waters. Suddenly, without turning his head, the Old Sailor said,

"An' how many toots did that 'ere fog-horn give?"

"Two," replied Henry.

"An' what do that mean?"

"That the vessel is on the port tack."

"Werry good, too. But how kin she tack w'en there ain't wind enough to blow out a match?" And the Old Sailor leaned back and laughed in his customary silent manner. Then, without any further prelude, he broke out thus: "I'm a bloomin' sojer ef this ain't the werry identical kind o' a fog wot it happened in."

"What?" cried both boys.

"That 'ere's edzackly wot I'm a-goin' fur to tell ye ef ye'll jess hold your breath till I kin git started. I were down on my luck putty consid'able at the time wot I'm a-speakin' of, an' I didn't seem to be able to git no sort o' a berth at all. So I sez to myself, sez I, 'Preehaps ef I try another port, I'll do better,' jess like that, me bein' aground in London. So I ups an' ships afore the mast on the bark *Sago Puddin'*, bound for Rio with a cargo o' quill tooth-picks, molasses, ready-made pants, and other knick-knacks. The second mate he sees I

4

were a old hand, an' so he puts me in the foretop,
w'ich the same I were werry well satisfied with.
Waal, we didn't have nothin' excitin', barrin' a
collision with a fishin'-smack off Goodwin Sands, a
gale o' wind off the Azores, a water-spout in latitood 26° north an' longitood 68° west, an' a small
matter o' six days' doldrums; howsumever, the doldrums isn't excitin'."

" What are doldrums?" asked George.

"Doldrums, my son, is nothin'. That are, it's
w'en there ain't no wind at all, an' you jess bug-
galug aroun', an' putty nigh tie your t'-gallant masts
into knots a-rollin'. Waal, as I were a-sayin' w'en
you interrupted me, we didn't have nothin' else
excitin' till we runs into the blam'dest, thickest,
oiliest fog wot I ever seed. This 'ere one makes
me think on't, but it ain't so heavy. Why, the fog
was so thick the cap'n couldn' tell time by his
watch on deck, 'cos w'y : w'en he were lookin' at
the minnit hand, he couldn't see as fur as the hour
hand. Ef you stuck your hand out in front o' you,
it 'd git lost in the fog jess ez ef it 'd b'en bit off.
Waal, the cap'n he got a notion into his head that
it were a-comin' on to blow, an' he sends hands
aloft to furl the t'-gallant-s'ls. I went up on the
fore-t'-gallant yard an' sot to work. Blow me fur
pickles, ef I didn't get all mixed up 'cos I couldn't
see nothin' a foot away from me. So, as luck would
have it, I went out on the yard-arm, w'en I thort I
were a-goin' in towards the mast, an' fust thing I

knowed I went off the bloomin' thing an' ca-plunk into the sea. Somebody heard me go, an' hove a life-buoy over the side, at the same time a-yellin' 'Man overboard!' loud enough fur to bust hisself, only it were Bill Smock, an' he had lungs made o' rawhide.

"Waal," said the Old Sailor, after a momentary pause, "they lowered away a boat, but they didn't dare go werry fur from the ship fur fear she'd never find the way back agin. I kep' a-hollerin' an' a-swimmin', but I could hear from the sounds o' their voices w'en they hollered back that I were a-gittin' further away all the time. This lasted about an hour, an' I were gittin' mighty tired an' mighty skeered, 'cos w'y : I couldn't hear no more shoutin'. Then I felt a bit of a breeze. Ten minnits later the fog broke, an' I saw the bark about three-quarters o' a mile away. All her boats was at the davics, so I knowed they'd gave me up. Sure 'nuff, as soon as the breeze fairly filled her sails, she squared away on her course.

"Boys, it were not a agreeable position fur a honest, hard - workin' sailor. Howsumever, I didn't quite despair, 'cos w'y : about a hundred yards away I sees the life-buoy. I swimmed to it an' got it over my head an' down under my arms. 'Now,' sez I to myself, sez I, 'I'm werry comf'table purwidin' no onconsiderate shark comes along an' bites off my legs.' Jess as I had said that I seed a shark's fin not more 'n two hundred yards away. I decided

that my number were h'isted an' I were bound fur
Davy Jones's locker. But while I were a-watchin'
the fin I were jess paralyzed to see a hand come up
out o' the water an' catch hold o't. An' the hand
were followed by a head with a plug-hat on't. The
head took a glance around, an' seein' me, ducked
under like a shot. It come up agin in a minnit, an'
tuk another look. Then it went down, the hand
followin'. The next second the bloomin' thing
comes up right alongside o' me, an' stares into
my face. Waal, I were some flabbergasted, but I
couldn' help laffin'. This 'ere pusson's face were
so funny. He looked like one o' them pictures o'
Irishmen wot you see in a comic paper, on'y his
eyes an' the beard aroun' his neck was green.

"'Wot are you a-laffin' at?" sez he to me, sez he.

"'Beggin' your pardin',' sez I to him, sez I, 'but
you are the livin' image o' Teddy Mulcahey, wot
wore fust mate o' the *Smokin' Sarah*, an' were
drowned. Are you him?'

"'No, I are not him,' sez he to me, sez he; 'my
name are Benjamin B. Seagrave, an' I never were a
sailor, 'cos I are by birth an' perfession a merman.'

"'Oh,' sez I, 'then you 'ain't got no legs?'

"'Legs! No, certingly not. Wot good is legs out
here in one thousand seven hundred fathom o' water?'

"'Not havin' no legs,' sez I, 'you ain't afraid o'
havin' em bit off.'

"'Bit off! What in water are you a-talkin'
about? Oh, I see. You're a-lookin' at my shark.'

"'WOT ARE YOU A-LAFFIN' AT?' SEZ HE TO ME, SEZ HE"

"'Oh, are that your shark!'

"'Yes; he's all right. He wouldn't bite you.'

"'I wouldn't like to give him a chance.'

"'Here, Fido! here, Fido! here, Fido!' he calls, and the shark comes a-swimmin' up a-waggin' his tail. 'You go right home, sir,' sez Mr. Seagrave, 'an' mind, this 'ere gen'leman are a friend o' mine, an' he's not to be bit.'

"The shark he waggles his tail some more, stands on his head, an' goes straight down.

"'W'ere do you live?' sez I to Mr. Seagrave.

"'Oh, jess below here,' he sez, pointin' down.

"'How fur?' sez I.

"'A little over three-quarters o' a mile,' sez he. 'Come down an' I'll interdooce ye to my wife.'

"'No, thankee,' sez I.

"'Oh, o' course,' sez he, 'I forgot. You'd git drownded. Say, wot are you doin' here anyhow? Workin' fur the coast survey?'

"'Nah; fell overboard from the bark *Sago Puddin'*.'

"Waal, Mr. Seagrave he jess leaned back an' shuck his sides a-laffin'. W'en he got his wind agin, he sez to me, sez he:

"'I've heerd tell o' razor-clam puddin', an' octopus-puddin' with squid sass, but wot 'n gracious are sago-puddin'?'

"I allowed that I didn't rightly know myself, never havin' eat the same. An' then I sez to him, sez I:

"'I wouldn't mind havin' some now, 'cos w'y: I'm feelin' a leetle chilly an' putty consid'able hungry.'

"'Waal, you jess come along o' me,' sez he, 'an' I'll fix you up.'

"He were a-startin' to dive down w'en I ketched him by the lapel o' his coat an' hinted to him that I couldn't dive down quite so deep.

"'Oh, I keep a-forgettin',' sez he to me, sez he, 'that you're one o' them there poor shore pussons. Howsumever, we kin soon manage. I know a nice little coral reef not fur from here. It's out o' water at low tide, an' we can lie on the reef an' eat. I'll jess call my carridge.'

"So sayin' he stuck his head down under the water an' made a noise wot sounded edzackly like the ringin' o' a bell. I dunno how he did it, but he did. In about two minutes a rousin' big sword-fish, hitched to a big sea-shell, came up, an' Mr. Seagrave invited me to git in, w'ich the same I done.

"'Who's goin' to drive?' sez I.

"'We don't drive. We jess talks fishy to him, an' he knows w'ere to go.'

"So he leans over the dash-board an' sez somethin' to the sword-fish, an' away we went a-whizzin'. Wall, we got to the coral reef all right 'nuff, an' the carridge were sent below agin, he havin' said somethin' to the fish. In three or four minutes I see a b'ilin' in the water, an' up comes a merwoman, follered by a lot o' little merlads an' mermaids.

"'These here,' sez Mr. Seagrave, 'is my wife an' fam'ly.'

"I bowed to 'em, and they all flopped around an' laid out on the coral. Mrs. Seagrave were not wot you might call putty, seein' she were a werry sickly green with dark blue freckles, but the kids was kind o' spry an' cunnin'.

"'Are the dinner comin'?' sez Mr. Seagrave.

"Yes; Sally are a-bringing of it,' sez his wife.

"'Sally's our hired gal,' sez he to me; 'she are a Sally Growler, but we calls her jess plain Sally.'

"W'en she come up I seed that she were werry plain Sally. Howsumever, the dinner were plainer still, bein' as how it were all raw. But I filled myself up with three oysters."

"With three?" exclaimed Henry.

"Yep," responded the Old Sailor. "W'y, they wos as big as your two fists, an' a dozen on 'em would 'a' fed a small fam'ly. Waal, the more I looked at this 'ere fam'ly o' merpeople the more I thought I could make a everlastin' fortune ef I could get 'em to go ashore with me an' exhibit in a dime museum. So I sez to Mr. Seagrave, says I:

"'Ever b'en ashore?'

"'W'y,' sez he to me, sez he, 'I'm ashore now, ain't I?'

"'Oh, I mean on land—in America, fur instance.'

"'Yes,' he sez, 'once w'en I were young.'

"'Wouldn't you like to go back?' sez I.

"'No,' sez he.

"'But s'posin' I could make it wuth your while.'

"'I don't see how you could,' sez he, thortfullike; 'w'y, fur one thing there's no water ashore, an' I 'ain't got nothin' to walk with.'

"'But s'posin' I was to agree to furnish you with a big tank full o' salt water, an' with glass sides so you could see out.'

"Mrs. Seagrave an' the children sot up an' looked werry sharp at me, an' Mr. Seagrave sez, werry slow,

"'Wot do you mean?'

"'Waal,' sez I to him, sez I, not knowin' no better, 'ef I could have you an' your fam'ly on exhibition fur about a year, I could make a hundred thousan' dollyers, an' I'd give you half, an' then you—'

"But at that moment Mrs. Seagrave an' the kids let out a awful screech an' dived into the sea with a loud splash. Mr. Seagrave, whose green face had turned to a sickly yaller, sez to me:

"'I might 'a' knowed better 'n to talk to a bloomin' landlubber. All you people want o' us is to catch one o' us an' show him in a tank. But you 'ain't never done it yet, an' you never will. You make sham mermaids an' show 'em, but you 'ain't never had a real one. All my life I've been watchin' out ag'in schemes o' you landlubbers to catch me, an' I b'en eddicatin' up my children to look out for 'em, too. An' now, by the great whale's fin, I find you a-floatin' out here in the middle o' the sea in danger o' starvin', I treat you decent, an' give you somethin' to eat, an' right off you want to get me into a tank an' make a show o' me. That ever I should have lived to see the day! Annyhow, you're the first landlubber that ever had a face-to-face talk with one o' us, an' you're a-goin' to be the last.'

"With that he grabbed me round the neck an' dove into the sea. I made up my mind I were a-goner. Down, down we went, till arter a while he sez in my ear—an' I could hear him under water too —'Now drown, you landlubber!' With that he lets me go, an' he disappears. I couldn't hold my breath no longer, so I *opened* my mouth, swallowed water, an' fainted. W'en I come to I were floatin' around in the sea. 'Cos w'y: I still had the life-buoy on, an' it 'd brung me up to the top. But I were crazy as a loon for two weeks arter I were picked up by the steamer *Consolation*, bound from Cape Town to Barnegat, New Jersey, with a cargo o' Dutch cheese, an' I couldn't do nothin' 'cept lie in a bunk an' holler one thing."

"What?" cried the boys.

"He called me a landlubber!"

Then the fog began to lift, and the boys went home to dinner.

It was a cold and cheerless morning. The wind piped icily out of the northwest, sending clouds of dust swirling off the well-beaten road that ran near the beach. The sky was nearly overcast with big leaden-colored tufted clouds with white edges, between which here and there the blue sky showed in gloomy rifts. The sea was of a dull, leaden tint, and under the lee of the shore it was smooth. Far out, however, sharp-cornered waves could be seen against the distant horizon, and the two or three schooners in sight were boiling along in great smothers of foam under double-reefed mainsails, single-reefed foresails, and small jibs. Henry and his little brother were looking with interest at the sea, when they saw the Old Sailor approaching.

"Mornin'," he said. "Fine blowin' weather."

"Yes," said Henry; "it does blow, and it's cold, too."

"It generally are cold in winter," said the Old Sailor, laughing one of his silent laughs. "Mebbe you've noticed that."

Henry laughed, and admitted that he had.

"But s'posin'," said the Old Sailor, "I wos to

go fur to ask you w'y it war cold, wot 'd you say ?"

"It's cold because it's winter," said Henry.

"An' w'y is 't winter ?"

"Because the sun has gone south, and it's summer below the equator."

"Werry good, too," commented the Old Sailor; "you'll be a man some day, sure. S'posin' now I wos to go fur to ask you w'ich way were the wind, wot 'd you say ?"

"I'd say about northwest."

"Not so werry bad, 'cos it's nor'west an' by west." The Old Sailor was silent for a minute, and then he continued : "S'posin' I wos to go fur to say to you has your mother any hot coffee, wot 'd you say ?"

"I'd say yes."

"An' s'posin' I wos to say would she give some to an Old Sailor purwidin' as how he'd tell her two boys a yarn ?"

"Of course she would. Come right along."

And they led the Old Sailor to their home, where he was soon seated in a corner by a roaring fire, drinking the hot coffee. He looked thoughtfully at the blaze in front of him, shook his head, set down the empty cup, and said :

"It were in the winter o' 1849 that I were shut up in a hospitual with some kind o' a disconcertion o' my pussonal health, o' w'ich the name I are forgetful. Howsumever, w'en I got out I were so tired o' bein' shut up that I'd 'a' shipped fur Bendigo in a flour-sieve. Wot I did ship in were the bark *Molly Prism*, bound from New York fur Iceland fur a cargo o' ice."

"Why, I never heard of a ship's going to Iceland for ice," exclaimed Henry.

"Waal, you hear o' 't now," said the Old Sailor, gravely. "The ice-crop here were a failer, an' w'ere should you go for ice 'ceptin' to the land o' 't? But that 'ain't got nothin' to do with the yarn wot I'm a-goin' fur to tell you. The *Molly Prism* were a reg'lar old trap, she were. The only good p'int she had were that she didn't have rats. 'Cos why?— no rat 'd be such a fool as to go to sea in her. How she ever got so fur away from the Romer Beacon as latitude 70° are more 'n I kin rightly explain, 'ceptin' that we had bath-tub weather all the time. We passed out by Sandy Hook Light-ship with a fair an' gentle sou'west breeze, an' we carried that with us almost up to Georges Bank. Then it veered to the west'rd, an' give us a good sailin' breeze fur nigh on to forty-eight hours, so that the bloomin' old hooker made nine knots an hour, w'ich fur her were lightnin' speed.

"Waal," continued the Old Sailor, after a moment of silent reflection, "this here fine weather couldn't last forever, 'cos fine weather never do. So one day the cap'n comes on deck an' sees a awful lot o' copper-colored clouds in the sou'east, an' says he to the mate, says he, 'How's yer byrometer?' An' the mate says to him, says he, 'It's werry wob-

bly, sir,' says he, just like that. 'Then,' says the
cap'n to him, says he, 'We're a-goin' fur to have a
gale o' wind, an' nawthin' else, right out o' the sou'-
east; so stand by an' get the cloth off her.' So
we wos all turned to a-gettin' in sail, an' at the same
time it fell a dead calm, an' the sea looked like molasses turned green, 'cos it were so slick an' smooth.
The swell come in from the sou'east soon after, an'
fur eight hours we wallered an' rolled, till I actially
thort as how the masts 'd snap off close to the deck.
W'y, some o' the youngsters wot hadn' been to sea
more 'n ten or twelve year wos sea-sick. Then the
wind come in, an', Lord bless you, how it did blow!
In about two hours there were a awful sea runnin',
an' it didn' get no better. Contrairiwise, it growed
wusser an' wusser, till I thort that there old *Molly
Prism* were a-goin' to roll over an' over an' over like
a ball.

"Waal, I knowed the *Molly Prism* wouldn't stand
it werry long. She were a-creakin' an' a-groanin'
like a old man wi' the lumbager. After about six
hours o' the gale there were a big crash, an' she bruk
in two right in the middle. We all cried out in our
fright, but cryin' out didn' do no good. The next
minute the two halves o' the bark went all to pieces,
an' we wos scattered around on the howlin' sea. I
had the good-luck to be throwed by a wave ag'in' the
mainmast. There were lots o' riggin' hangin' to 't,
so I clumb up an' made myself fast. I never seen
nawthin' more o' the rest o' that ship's company,

though I heern tell that some on 'em wos picked up by a whaler an' carried to Upernavik. But that weren't my luck. I jess drifted an' drifted an' drifted fur I dunno how long. I were pretty nigh froze to death, an' were so hungry I chewed the tarred rope on the masts. After a while I got kind o' faint, an' didn' seem to know nawthin' much, till I were sort o' waked up by the mast poundin' ag'in' somethin'. An' wot d' ye s'pose the mast were bumpin' ag'in'?"

"What?"

"A iceberg about two hundred feet high." The Old Sailor paused for a moment and shook his head. "I didn' seem to think werry much o' the company I'd met, 'cos the sides o' the berg wos straight up an' down, an' the ice were hard enough to smash my mast all to splinters. But, as I were lookin' around a-wonderin' wot I could do, all on a sudden I spies a beautiful flight o' steps cut in the side o' the berg."

"What? Steps!" exclaimed the boys.

"That's wot I'm a-tellin' of," said the Old Sailor.

"Well," asked Henry, "what did you do?"

"Wot did I do? W'en a gen'leman is in fifteen hundred fathom o' ice-water, hangin' to a spar, an' he bumps up ag'in' a flight o' steps, wot does he do? He goes up 'em, says I, an' that's wot I done. It seemed a long way up, too, but I furgot all about that w'en I got to the top."

"Why?" asked the boys.

"'Cos I seen a little house o' snow on top o' the

berg, an' a Esquimau dog run out an' barked at me."

The boys were now breathless with astonishment, as the Old Sailor continued :

"As soon as the dog barked, a head popped up out o' the top o' the house and says, 'Hallo ! How d' ye do ?' Blow me fur pickels ef I warn't knocked clean silly to hear that there Esquimau talk United States. I stood there without a word to say, but he had lots. 'W'ere ye from, an' w'ere ye boun'?' says he to me, says he. 'I'm from the wreck o' the *Molly Prism*, an' I'm boun' to git ashore sommers,' says I to him, says I, just like that. 'I might 'a' knowed you,' says he to me. 'Come up an' shake han's, an' don't mind the dorg, 'cos he 'ain't got no teeth.' 'Wot !' says I, 'are it you ?' An' he allowed that it were."

"Who, who ?" cried the boys.

"My second cousin, Hiram Dorky, wot went to sea two years arter I did."

"And how did he come to be there ?"

"That's wot I'm a-goin' fur to tell you. Hiram took me in an' sets me down at the table, fur he were just at breakfast, an' he thort I must be hungry, w'ich were gospel truth. 'Wot 'll ye have ?' says he; 'there's fish, feesh, an' fishes.' • 'Not much wariety,' says I, 'about this, as the ole woman said w'en she were sea-sick.' 'It's wot I has three times a day,' says Hiram, ''ceptin' once in a w'ile w'en I gets a stray bird aboard o' my berg.' 'Is this your berg?'

says I. 'Course,' says he. 'Oh,' says I, 'I didn't know but you mought 'a' stole it out o' some gen'leman's back yard!' 'Waal,' says he, 'not edzackly; and yit putty nigh.' So then he ups an' tells me. Hiram were with a whaler, and she got shut in the ice away up in Baffin's Bay. Hiram an' another feller went on a foragin' expedition, an' they fotched up in a Esquimau camp on the foot o' a glacier. They stayed there several days; an' Hiram's pard went out seal-huntin' one day, an' never come back. Hiram got so fond o' the Esquimaux that he settled down in their camp, an' lived there two years. One night he wos woke up by a loud crash, an' heard yells. He ran out, but it were darker 'n pitch, an' he couldn't see nothin'. He hollered, but nobody answered. He waited fur a while, and then started to go to his neighbor's house. Then he found wot he took to be a new crack in the ice. He were afraid to move any more, so he went back to his house an' waited for daylight, w'ich came along about three weeks arter. An' then he diskivered that he were floatin' in the open sea on a berg. The crash had been w'en the berg bruk off'n the glacier. An' he'd been floatin' fur six weeks w'en he met me travellin' the same way."

"And what did you do?"

"Now we come to the sad part o' this here tale," said the Old Sailor, shaking his head and gazing mournfully into the fire. "That there berg, as nigh as I kin reckon, had drifted around, an' had

"'HALLO! HOW D' YE DO?'"

at last got into the sou'erly current wot sets down
from the pole. She begin to drift to the sou'ard,
an' the weather begin to get milder. Hiram he
sweat and puffed, an' got whiter every day.

"'Tain't no use,' says he to me, says he, one day;
'I can't stand this heat.' You see, he'd been a-livin'
in a cold country so long. Waal, to make the story
short, we got down into the roarin' forties byme-by,
an' our berg run aground on the Gran' Banks o'
Newfoundland. An' one day, w'en it were dead
calm an' hotter'n blue blazes, Hiram keeled over
sunstruck. Waal, I were all alone on the berg, 'ceptin' fur the dog; an' the next day the heat druv
him mad, an' he jumped into the sea an' swum out
o' sight. I thort I'd go crazy up there on that berg
in the next week, but somehow I didn't. One night
I were walkin' around on my lawn—made o' green
ice—w'en I spied the lights o' a steamer. It were
a werry thick night, an' I saw by the way she were
a-headin' that she were a-goin' to run bang into my
berg. So I run down the steps an' begin to holler:
'Keep off! Keep off there! Ef you smash my
berg I'll sue you.' W'en they got close enough they
heard me, an' they put their helm hard a-starboard
an' sheered off. Then they stopped the engines, and
the skipper guv me a hail. 'Who are you?' says he.
'I'm a sailor-man,' says I, 'an' I'm aground.' 'Waal,'
says he, 'hold on a minute an' I'll send a boat fur
you.' 'Much obleeged,' says I to him, says I, just
like that. An' so he sends a boat fur me, an' putty

5

soon I were aboard the tank-steamer *Isles o' Greece*, from Christiania fur Boston. An' wot d' ye think ?"

" What ?" breathlessly asked the boys.

" I'd been a-walkin' on ice so long I couldn't stand up on a wooden deck, an' I fell down an' bruk my arm."

And they all gazed gravely into the fire.

It was a clear and beautiful moonlight night in March. It was also a cold night. There was very little wind to speak of, but there was a biting crispness in the atmosphere, so that any one who was out for a walk felt like keeping up a pretty lively gait. Henry Hovey and his little brother had been studying their lessons, for school-days had come again, and they were not idle boys. When they had finished, a few minutes after eight o'clock, Henry looked out of the window, and exclaimed,

"I tell you, mother, this is a fine night!"

Mrs. Hovey looked out, and agreed with her son.

"Yes," added George; "and how dancy the stars are!"

"I feel dancy myself this sort of weather," said Henry. "Mother, mayn't we go out and run as far as the beach and back? It isn't bedtime yet."

"Yes," said Mrs. Hovey; "I think a breath of fresh air will make you sleep better."

"Hurrah!" cried George, snatching up his cap.

The next minute the two boys were bounding over the rough road towards the sea. It was only a short distance, and, according to their custom, they made straight for the old pier. They did not dream of finding the Old Sailor there; but he was there. He was not sitting down. He was standing on the end of the pier, gazing out to sea. He heard the boys' footsteps, and turned his head.

"Waal, waal, waal!" he exclaimed. "I wouldn't never 'a' thort o' seein' you out here at night."

"And we didn't expect to see you," replied Henry.

"I s'pose ye jess couldn' stay in no house w'en it were sich a werry fine night out-o'-doors."

"That's it. Mother said a breath o' fresh air would do us good."

"Mother said so, eh? That there mother o' yours —say, are she made any doughnuts to-day?"

"No; but there are some left from yesterday."

"Werry good, too; *werry*, werry good. An' d' ye s'pose there might be any tea-leaves in the pot?"

"Maybe."

"An' some hot water in the kittle?"

"Sure to be."

"Also werry good. I were a-thinkin' that p'rhaps you would sleep a little extry better ef you heard about wot this 'ere moonlight night reminded me of."

"Oh, I'm sure we would!" cried Henry.

"But this 'ere pier are not no bed o' down on sich a night, an' ef I were to keep you here a-tellin' o' a yarn I expect your mother wouldn't like it. Moreover, also, an' furthermore, you might git a sore throat."

"Then walk up to the house with us."

"That are about wot I were a-proposin' to do."

"And I'm sure mother will give you a doughnut and a cup of hot tea."

"W'ich the same would be werry agreeable on this 'ere cool evenin', an' I think might werry likely make the yarn a leetle longer."

So the three friends started for the house. On arriving there Henry explained the state of affairs to his mother, and the cup of tea and the doughnut were soon produced.

"Now," said Henry, "what were you thinking about when we found you?"

"W'ich the same I are about to relate to you in a plain an' simple tale o' the sea. It were a werry large an' old-fashioned ship wot I seed out there wot sot me a-thinkin' about a experience wot I had oncet on to a man-o'-war in furrin waters." The Old Sailor swallowed the last mouthful of tea, and then said: "Thankee, marm. The principal pussonage in this 'ere yarn wot I are a-goin' fer to tell you were a torpedo."

"A torpedo?"

"Yes. Not the kind wot boys throw at sea-farin' gen'lemen on the Fourth o' July, but the kind that is occupied aboard o' war-ships."

"What kind is that?"

"A torpedo are a kind o' a invention wot are made out o' copper an' other metal in the shape o' a cigar. It are loaded with gun-cotton or dynamite or some sich stuff to make it go off, an' it has machinery in it to turn a propeller wot makes it go jess like a boat. An' there's a wire to it w'ich the same you keep the end of aboard the ship, an' by electricity you steer the aforesaid, an' make it do 'most anythin', 'ceptin' to talk, w'ich it warn't never intended to do but oncet—an' then, good-bye. The puppose of a torpedo is to blow up a enemy's wessel. You launch the torpedo overboard, havin' started the machinery, an' away she goes at a 20-knot gait, you a-steerin' of her by the electric wire. W'en she hits the other ship you explodes her by electricity, an' the other ship goes to Davy Jones's locker in sections. Are that plain to your mind?"

"Oh yes," said the boys. "Now," added Henry, "tell us about your torpedo."

"Waal," said the Old Sailor, "it were in the Russo-Turkish war. I were knockin' around Europe without no berth w'en it bruk out, an' so I says to myself, says I, here's goin' to be a shindy with chances for prize-money, an' I hurried off an' 'listed. I were not a green hand edzackly, 'cause I'd sarved three years on the *Minnesota* an' one year on the *Hartford* durin' a diffikilty w'ich ariz betwixt the North'n and the South'n parts of the United States, in w'ich the same we live. Howsumever, I didn't speak any Roosian; but they put me on the cruiser *Skipoffvitch*, w'ere an ossifer wot talked English had charge o' the powder diwision; an' findin' I were an old American man-o'-war's man, he took me into his gang an' put me to work. Before the

war got fairly started I knowed all the commands
in Roosian; an' w'en a ossifer swalleyed his front
teeth, choked, coughed, an' said, 'Ouftik gouvitch-
sky vod,' I knowed putty well that he meant, 'Cast
loose and purwide,' w'ich is the order to git everythin' ready fur to load up and shoot.

"The business o' this 'ere cruiser *Skipoffvitch*
were pecul'ar an' aggrawatin'. I s'pose you know
that there are a passage o' water 'connectin' the
Black Sea with the Mediterranean, an' that the
Black Sea are chiefly inhabited by Roosians. Leastways, you ought to know it, an' if you don't, what
fur do you study geoggerfy, w'ich the same I s'pose
you have at school."

"Oh yes," said Henry; "and the strait you mean
is the Bosporus."

"W'ich the same it isn't," said the Old Sailor.
"The strait wot I'm alludin' to are the Dardanelles,
not the Bosporus. The *Skipoffvitch* were engaged
in hangin' around, dodgin' in an' out among the islands o' the Greek Archipelager for the purpose o'
prewentin' any Turkish man-o'-war from Constantinople from gittin' out an' away into the Mediterranean. There was plenty o' Roosian ships in the
Black Sea to head 'em off if they tried to run up to
Odessa or sich ports, an' we wanted to keep 'em
shut up in the Sea o' Marmora, w'ere they couldn't
do no harm to nothin' 'ceptin' their own perwisions.
Waal, to prewent this 'ere story from growin' as
long as our cruise, I'll jess skip over a month or so,

an' come down to the partikler occasion w'en that torpedo got lost. Fust and foremost lemme ask you w'ether you ever saw a dry gale o' wind?"

"You mean a gale when it doesn't rain, and the sun often comes out from behind the clouds?" said Henry. "Oh yes, I've seen that kind of a gale right here on this coast often."

"Werry good, too," said the Old Sailor, gazing out into the bright moonlight at the ships in the harbor, and laughing heartily, but without a sound. "Only in this 'ere gale wot I'm a-tellin' of the moon were more notable than the sun, 'cause what this story are about happened at night. It had been a-blowin' a howlin' dry gale fur two days, an' the cap'n allowed that it would be better fur us to go an' lie up under the lee o' a werry small an' low island jess outside o' the entrance to the Dardanelles, w'ere a lookout at the topmast head could see any wessel wot might try to come out, while our ship could be ridin' werry snug to her anchors. Bless you, how it war blowin'! The clouds were sizzlin' across the sky like great buckets full o' spray, an' every oncet in a while the moon would come shootin' out from behind one o' 'em like a white - hot cannon - ball. The sea were roarin' like ten thousand mad bulls, an' the combers were breakin' on every wave. To make things all the more interestin', the sea war alive with phosphorescence, an' every comber that broke looked as if she wos on fire. It were nigh on to the most grandest

night wot I ever seed at sea. Every time a sea
hit our cruiser under the bow the spray 'd fly up
around the catheads like flames, an' I'm blamed ef
it didn't make even me feel creepylike sometimes.
'Cos w'y? It didn't look real, it didn't, but more
like a sort o' a burnin' ghost o' a sea. Leastways,
that's wot I says to myself standin' right there
on the starboard side o' the forec's'le-deck of the
Roosian cruiser *Skipoffvitch.*

"Waal, we wos a-gittin' well up under the lee o'
the aforesaid island w'en the lookout let us know
that he seed a sail, w'ich the same looked like a
man-o'-war. One o' the ossifers went aloft an' took
a look, an' then he came down in a great deal o' a
hurry, an' after that there wos a great lot o' whis-
perin' among the ossifers on the quarter-deck. Putty
soon some orders wos gave, an' I made out that the
wessel comin' out war steerin' such a course that
she'd pass close around the south end o' the island,
an' not more 'n seven hundred yards from w'ere we
were a-proposin' to anchor. The cap'n's idee were
that she wouldn't see us in behind the island, an'
she'd be right on top o' us afore she knowed anythin',
an' we'd just blow her into flinders with a torpedo.
I didn't think it were much o' a night fur torpedo
practice, but as I weren't an ossifer, but a seaman,
I were not supposed to think. There warn't no
question about her bein' a Turk, 'cos none o' our
ships from the Black Sea could 'a' got through the
Bosporus noway at all.

"The torpedo were got ready, an' I stood by with the rest o' the launchin' crew. We waited an' waited, an' putty soon, arter we'd waited about an hour, the ship hove in sight off the point. She were a great high‑sided, old‑fashioned hooker, an' she were a sort o' a greenish-white, like moonlight, or a iceberg at night, from water-line to truck. I tell you, boys, that there wessel gave me the shivers the werry minnit I see her. An', bless you! although it war blowin' a gale, that craft had every stitch o' canvas set ; yet she were a-creepin' along like she war tired. The torpedo ossifer he didn't seem to notice nothin', but give the order, an' the torpedo were launched.

"We could see it rushin' thro' the seas jess as plain as if it were day, on account o' the phosphores-cence an' the moonlight, an' I says to myself, says I, that the other ship would see it too, an' would let loose on it with her rapid-fire guns, ef she had any. But blow me for a porpoise ef she paid any atten-tion at all to it. 'They're all asleep,' says our cap'n, laughin', 'an' in a second they'll all be in eternity.' Our torpedo ossifer were fairly dancin', he were so excited. The torpedo were steerin' beautiful, an' war goin' as straight fur the ship as a bullet at a target on shore. The wire were runnin' out at a sixteen-knot gait, an' the electric sharp stood by to press the key w'en he got the order. In a few short seconds we saw the torpedo right under the strange wessel's side.

"'WE COULD SEE IT RUSHIN' THRO' THE SEAS JESS AS PLAIN AS
IF IT WERE DAY'"

" ' Ouamphkth !' screeched the torpedo ossifer.

" The electric feller pushed down the key, an' we all held our breaths, a-lookin' at the stranger an' waitin fur the explosion.

" Pst ! That there wessel went out."

" Did what ?" exclaimed the boys.

" Went out—jess like gas wot's turned off. There warn't no explosion at all ; not a sound ; but the icebergy-lookin' ship warn't there. That's all."

" But the torpedo ?"

" That weren't there, either. The wire fell slack an' stopped runnin' out, an' w'en we hauled it all in the end were jess burnt off, an' smelled like all the brimstone in creation 'd got on to it. We had to chuck it overboard, or else the hull crew 'd been suffercated."

" And what became of the white ship ?"

" My young friend, there is some questions wot can't be answered."

" But what was she ?"

" It ain't fur me to say wot she were," said the Old Sailor, very gravely, " but it 's allus been my solemn conwiction that them there Roosians tried to torpedo the *Flyin' Dutchman*, w'ich the same you can't."

He was a queer-looking fellow. His hair was fiery red, and stuck out in ragged wisps under the rim of his slouched hat. His shaggy red eyebrows hung bristling over a pair of cold, steely gray eyes that seemed to swim in moisture. His nose had evidently been broken, and that very badly, for it was a shapeless mass. His beard, like his hair, was brilliant, and it looked as if it had never known a comb. His face was deathly pale, and his gaze was fixed straight ahead. His hands were clasped loosely behind the tails of his threadbare brown coat, and he had a large green handkerchief wound around his neck.

The Old Sailor sat watching him as he passed gravely down the street. Then he shook his head, shuddered as if he had a chill, and said, "S'posin' I wos to ax you fur a glass o' suthin' hot?"

"I think I could get it," said Henry.

"Thankee kindly," said the Old Sailor. "Ye see, I've ben kind o' friz up by wot I've seed."

"Do you mean the man that went down the street?"

"Did you see him?"

"Certainly I saw him."

"It were him," continued the Old Sailor, musing-ly, as he sipped his "suthin' hot"—"it were him sure. Now I wonder wot do he want here?"

"Who is he?" asked Henry.

"Well, it are consid'able of a tale, it are ; an' then, w'en it are all done, ye don't know who he are no more nor I do, w'ich the same I were shipmates with him ; leastways he were my passinger fur three weeks."

"Oh, tell me about it!"

"That are edzackly wot I'm a-preparin' fur to do. O' course we'll have a gale o' wind inside o' twenty-four hours; 'cos w'y, he allus are bound to bring bad luck. It were w'en I were master o' the brigantine *Flyin'-Squirrel* that I got, as ye might say, acquainted with that 'ere individooal wot have jess passed by. I can't say as acquainted are edzackly the word, 'cos nobody can't never get to know no sich persons as them. 'Cos why, he are not a livin' bein'."

"A ghost?" exclaimed both boys.

"Jess as sure as a flyin'-fish are not a monkey," said the Old Sailor, gravely. "Jess listen to this 'ere yarn wot I'm a-goin' fur to tell ye, an' see ef any livin' bein' could 'a' behaved the way that 'ere critter did aboard my brigantine. The *Flyin'-Squirrel* were bound from St. John to Greenock, with a cargo o' carpet-tacks an' bottled beer. We got under way with as fine a whole-sail breeze over the port quarter as I ever seed, an' I laid a good course fur our desti-

nation. We bowled along at a 'leven-knot gait fur
about twenty hours out o' the fust day, an' then she
fell calm. It were a mean, measly calm, with a
cross-grained, hump-backed swell that rolled us scuppers under an' made the masts snap like whips. An'
hot! My eye! W'y, the werry water wot run in
through the scuppers 'd go up in steam off the decks.
Well, at noon I got the sun, an' found we'd made
two hundred and fourteen miles, so I wasn't so werry
mad about the calm, purwidin' it weren't goin' to
last long. Sure 'nuff, about four bells in the afternoon watch—wot shore folks calls two o'clock fur
short—I seed a blue-black cloud a-risin' in the sou'-
west, an' sez I to myself, sez I, 'We're a-goin' fur
to have all the wind we wants.' So I had all the
fore-an'-aft canvas taken in, an' put the brigantine
under her fore-tops'l an' a storm-jib. I hadn't no
more'n got this done than down it come all a-whoop-
in', rain fust an' wind — gallons of 't — behind. I
jumped below into my cabin to get my oilers, an' in
the far corner I seed a man sittin'. I thought it were
the steward, an' I shouts at him, 'Git forrard out o'
that, ye lubber, an' don't be a-luxooriatin' in here!'
With that I bounces on deck agin, 'cos 'twarn't no
kind o' time fur the skipper to be buggaluggin'
aroun' down below.

"Well, I ain't goin' fur to detain ye with no account o' that squall, 'cos one squall at sea are werry
much like another, 'ceptin' that the one you're in are
allus wuss than them wot ye remembers. Howsum-

ever, that ain't got nothin' to do with this 'ere yarn wot I'm a-tellin' you. As soon as it were over, I told the mate to put cloth on her, an' then I went below to git a dry pair o' boots an' to fill my pipe. As soon as I went into the cabin I seed that feller still a settin' there. I walked right up to him, an' then I seed it weren't the steward. It were that critter wot preambleated down this 'ere identical street not more'n ten minutes ago."

The Old Sailor paused to note the effect of this statement on his listeners, and finding it satisfactory, continued :

"'Who 'n Jerusalem are you?' sez I to him, sez I.

"'Wot's that to you?' sez he to me, sez he.

"'A good deal,' sez I, kinder flabbergasted by his answer, 'seein' as how I are the skipper o' this 'ere craft.'

"'Oh,' sez he, 'you're the skipper, eh? Well, I are a-goin' to Greenock with you.'

"'But,' sez I, stammerin' in my supprise, 'we don't take no passingers aboard this 'ere brig.'

"'You're a-takin' me,' sez he, grinnin'; 'an' as you wos two hundred and fourteen miles out at noon, I don't see how you kin put me ashore.'

"'H-h-how 'n bloomin' fun 'd ye git here?' I axed him.

"'Oh, never mind,' sez he ; 'here I are, an' I got money to pay fur my passidge. How much?'

"Well, I were so kerflummuxed that I jess up an' sez that I'd take him fur fifty dollars.

" ' How 'll ye have 't?' sez he to me, sez he — ' in big bills, little bills, er silwer ?'

" ' I'll take 't in gold, ef it's all the same to you,' sez I to him, sez I, jess like that, bein' a little mad now.

"Well, blow me fur pickles ef he didn't jess reach out an empty hand an' get two twenty-dollar gold pieces an' a ten right out o' the air !

" ' There's yer money,' sez he to me, a-smilin' like a dried mermaid in a mooseum. An' I were so silli-fied that I couldn't say a bloomin' word.

" ' Wot's yer name ?' sez I to him, sez I, a-bracin' up arter a while like a ship wot's bin knocked down by a squall.

" ' Well,' sez he to me, sez he, ' they used to call me Horatio B. Smiggs, an' I s'pose it. ain't furbid fur me to use that there same name now,' sez he, jess like that, me bein' the cap'n o' the brigantine, an' him a red-headed critter a-sittin' on to a locker.

" So I dooly entered him as a passinger tuk aboard at St. John; 'cos w'y, nobody would 'a' b'lieved me ef I'd said he come aboard out there in latitood an' longitood. I were putty consid'able hungry by this time, an' the steward comin' in with my dinner, I axed the new passinger to jine me in a social bite. ' No, thankee,' sez he to me ; ' I never eat.'

" An' with that he gits up an' goes on deck. I knowed the crew would be a-puzzlin' their bloomin' brains about him, an' I knowed how ready sailors wos to be sooperstigious. So I bolted my dinner an' went on deck. Sure enough, there were Horatio B. Smiggs a-walkin' up an' down the port side o' the quarter-deck, an' the han's forrard a-p'intin' at him an' lookin' werry curious. So I jess sez to the mate, sez I, 'This 'ere gen'leman's Mr. Smiggs, a passinger wot come aboard jess afore we sot sail.'

"'No, I didn't,' sez he; 'I come aboard jes afore that squall busted on ye. Cap'n, ye hadn't ort to go fur to deceive an honest man like your mate.'

"Waal, wot 'n goodness blue could I say? The mate looked scared, an' one o' the men wot were at the w'eel an' heerd the conversationin' looked scareder. So I jess winked at the mate an' tapped my head, meanin' to indicify that the passinger were crazy. Blow me fur pickles ef he didn't seem to see me, though his back were turned, for he wheeled around, winked at the mate, an' sez he : 'Don't you b'lieve him. I'm not crazy ; I'm dead.' An' then he laughs fit to bust hisself. I tell you he give me cold shivers all down my back. An' he scared the other men too. It weren't an hour later w'en I heerd one o' them a-sayin' to another, 'There won't be nothin' but bad luck on this 'ere v'yage, 'cos we got a spook aboard.'

"Well," continued the Old Sailor, after a momentary pause, " at four bells in the fust watch— wot shore folks calls ten o'clock at night — I heerd a fearful yell on deck an' a splash in the water, follered by the cry o' 'man overboard.' I jumped on deck jess in time to see somethin' a-slippin' away

c

astern.   Quick as I could I had the brigantine
brought to an' a boat lowered away.   Meantime I'd
learned that it were my bloomin' passinger.   He'd
bin walkin' on the rail, an' dancin' jigs there, an'
gin'rally scarin' the crew ; but all on a suddint he
slipped an' went over.   I tuk command o' the boat
myself, an' away we went.   O' course I were sure
he'd be sunk long afore we could git to him.   But
by the great horn spoon ! D' ye think ye kin drown
a dizzy ghost ?   Not much.   Putty soon we hears
him a-singin' :

> " ' Sittin' on the ocean,
> Underneath the stars,
> Waitin' fur a boat that's
> Rowed by jolly tars.'

"Sure 'nuff, w'en we come up to him he were
actooally a - sittin' on the ocean, with his feet
hangin' over—or I ort to say under — an' a-smokin'
a pipe wot smelled like brimstone.

"'How are ye, cap'n ?' he sez.   'I've gone an'
got my feet wet, an' now I s'pose I'll have rheu-
matiz agin.'

"He climbed into the boat an' sot down alongside o' me, an' blow me fur pickles ef he weren't as
dry as a hot biscuit, w'ich the same your cook
makes better'n any one on 'arth.   Thankee kindly,
lad ; since you're so pressin'.   I will eat one w'en
I've finished tellin' this 'ere yarn.   Well, arter that
there weren't no doin' nothin' with the crew at all.

I heerd one on 'em a-sayin' to another, 'We're gone an' got a Jonah aboard, an' we can't do no good throwin' him overboard, 'cos w'y, he won't git drownded ef we do.' Then the other sailor-man he sez, sez he: 'Wot kin we do? We kin jess go ahead an' work the ship into port as fast as ever we kin, an' that's all as we kin do,' sez he, jess like that. As fur me, I jess took Horatio B. Smiggs down in the cabin, an' sez I to him, sez I:

"'See here; ef you jump overboard agin, I'll sail right on an' leave you.'

"'Leave an' be blowed!' sez he; 'd' ye think there ain't no other wessel a-sailin' this 'ere ocean 'ceptin' yours? I reckon I kin git another passidge.'

"'Then I jess wish you'd go an' do 't,' sez I.

"'Oh, I'm werry comf'table right 'ere,' sez he.

"An' of course that settled it, an' I had to let him stay. He didn't make no more trouble till midnight. Then I were woke up by a great flappin' o' canvas, an' I knowed the brigantine were up in the wind. I jumped up an' went on deck. Fust thing I see were the man at the wheel, w'ich the same he were not at the wheel, but were hidin' behind the lee side o' the cabin.

"'Wot's up, mate?' sez I.

"'Ugh-h-hoo-hoo! Loo-oo-ook! sez he, p'intin.'

"Waal, I looked, an' there were that bloomin' passinger a-walkin' up an' down the middle o' the deck, an' walkin' right straight through the masts without seemin' to notice they wos there. I went up to him, an' sez I to him, sez I :

"'Look here, wot sort o' conduck do you call this?'

"'W'y,' sez he to me, sez he, 'it's the right sort. I'm a ghost, an' its arter midnight, so it's my business to walk.'

"'Yes,' sez I, 'but ye don't need to walk right through the masts that way an' scare the crew.'

"'I don't care who gets scared. Ghosts never do,' sez he.

"'Werry good,' sez I; 'then your walk are a-goin' fur to end right here.'

"With that I made a grab an' got hold o' his green silk neckerchief. He squealed an' pulled an' tried to git away, but 'twarn't no good. I jess yanked him down into the hold, an' tied him to a ring-bolt by his own necktie; an' then I sez to him, sez I, 'Good-night, sleep tight, an' don't let the rats bite.' Then I went back to my cabin an' turned in. I hadn't slep' more'n an hour w'en I were woke up agin, an' it were by the most terrifyin' o' all cries at sea—'Fire! fire!'

"Waal, I were on deck in less 'n a second, an' givin' orders to man the pumps an' do other things. Then I seed that the smoke were comin' right out o' the main-hatch, an' I remembered that Smiggs were down in the hold. I s'pected that he were at the bottom o' the trouble; so callin' to a hand to foller me, I jumps down. Well, blow me fur a salt mackerel ef that bloomin' Smiggs weren't sittin'

"'JEST YOU SHUT ME UP, AN' THEN YOU MAKE A ROW 'COS I SMOKE. IT'S TOUGH'"

there a-smokin' a great big pipe. The pipe were red-hot, an' Smiggs's eyes were a-blazin' like two hot coals; an', my lands! but you'd ort to seen the clouds an' clouds o' hot yallerish smoke wot wos a-comin' out o' that 'ere pipe!"

"'Say, Mr. H. B. Smiggs,' sez I, 'this 'ere's a-goin' too fur.'

"'What's the matter now?' sez he. 'Fust you shut me up, an' then you make a row 'cos I smokes. It's tough, that's wot it is. I'm a respectable, peace-lovin' ghost, an' all I axes are to be let alone.'

"Waal, some o' the men had follered me down, an' they was putty mad. 'Kill him!' yells one. 'Ye can't,' sez another. 'I'll have a hack at him anyhow,' says number one, an' afore I knowed wot were the matter he hauled off an' smashed the ghost in the face. Waal, it knocked Horatio B. Smiggs ag'in' the side o' the brigantine, an' blow me ef he didn't laff, an' go right on through into the water, leavin' a hole six feet high. O' course the water come a-rushin' in, an' we all hurried on deck to take to the boats, fur we knowed the brigantine would go down in a werry few minutes. It were a nice how-dy-do to be wrecked four hundred mile from shore by a bloomin' ghost wot were not inwited aboard, but there we was. We'd hardly got a few needfuls chucked into the long-boat an' got her lowered away w'en the *Flyin'-Squirrel* gives a lurch an' goes down slowly, her bow settlin' first. An' then what d' ye think happened?"

"What?" asked Henry.

"That 'ere measly spook appeared sittin' on the main-truck, smokin' his pipe an' laffin' fit to bust hisself.

"'Ye'll ill-treat a ghost, will ye?' he yells. 'Next time ye git one aboard ye'd better take good care o' him. Whee-ee-oop! Here we go down, down, downy!'

"An' with that him an' the brigantine sank out o' sight, an' I never seed him agin till I seed him a-goin' down that 'ere blessed street half an hour ago."

The boys gazed down the street with the deepest interest.

IT was a fine gusty April day, with a cool nor'-west wind swirling the dust down over the edge of the bluff and into the boiling undertow. The breakers were all wrinkled and twisted around their crests, where the piping breeze caught them, and tossed their manes of spray backward into the glooming hollows behind them. They reared themselves slowly, and, toppling over in reeling curves, broke in dull, muffled booms, which sounded far away by reason of the wind's carrying the sound seaward. Three or four miles out a schooner-yacht returning from Hampton Roads was beating to the northward on short and long legs under housed top-masts, a single reefed main-sail, foresail, staysail, and jib. At every lunge forward into the oily-looking valleys ahead of her she tore the green water into white foam, which burst in clouds of smokelike spray over the weather-bow, keeping the foot of the staysail dripping with dewy gems of brine.

On the end of the pier sat the Old Sailor, watching her with grave approval.

"A werry putty boat, an' a werry putty hand at the hellum," he said to himself, yet half aloud.

"What did you say?" inquired a voice behind him.

Turning his head, the Old Sailor saw his two young friends, whose approach he had not heard. He repeated his words.

"Oh, you mean the yacht," said Henry.

"How might you know she are a yacht?" asked the mariner.

"By her looks," said Henry.

"Werry good, too," answered the Old Sailor, indulging in one of his quiet laughs. "That are about the same way as how I know that you are you."

The two boys sat down beside their queer old friend and waited. They knew that some kind of a yarn was cooking in his head, and they felt sure that it was going to be about yachting. Perhaps it would have been, but at this moment the ancient seafarer caught sight of something which changed the current of his thoughts. It was a curious dark mass which rose on the crest of a distant sea and then sank. It kept rising and sinking, just as if it were some living thing bobbing its head up and down.

"Now," said the Old Sailor, pointing at it, "What might that be?"

The two boys took a long and careful survey of the object, and finally Henry said, "It's an old spar, or something of that kind, floating."

"Looks as if it were alive," said his little brother.

"Werry good, indeed," said the Old Sailor, laughing. "Both on you is right. I've knowed some skippers wot 'd put that there spar down in the log as the sea-serpent."

"The sea-serpent!" exclaimed the boys.

"That's wot I said," gravely answered their friend.

"Why, there isn't any such thing, is there?" asked Henry.

"There used to be one; now there is four on 'em," was the remarkable answer.

"Four?"

"Them's it."

"Oh, please tell us about it."

"Waal," said the Old Sailor, crossing his legs, "this 'ere yarn wot I'm a-goin' to tell you happened w'en I were a man-o'-war's man, a-sarvin' o' the glorious flag o' our country aboard the United States ship *Chicago*, commanded by Actin' Rear-Admiral John G. Barker."

"Why, then it must have been not long ago," said Henry.

"Only a werry short time afore I quit the sea fur good," continued the Old Sailor. "I suppose mebbe you young gen'lemen has heerd o' the squadron o' evolution, wot went over to the other side o' the ocean to show the furriners that we wos a-gettin' a new navy."

"Yes," said Henry, "and I know the names of the ships, too— *Chicago*, *Boston*, *Atlanta*, and *Yorktown*."

"Werry good, too," said the Old Sailor. "Waal,

it were on that there cruise that this 'ere yarn wot I'm a-goin' fur to tell you happened to this 'ere identical sailor, likewise to all the other identical sailors in the fleet, includin' old Whiskers himself, an' also the marines.   We'd had a putty interestin' gale o' wind wot 'd made the little *Yawktown* — or *Corktown*, as we jackies used to call her—heave to, back end fust.   Arter that there gale were over we had putty fine weather, an' one handsome mornin' the admiral says he to himself, says he, 'It's bloomin' nigh time we begins to smell cigarettes.'   Cos w'y, he knowed we mus' be a-gettin' sommers near the coast o' Spain, an' them Spaniards has cigarettes fur breakfast, dinner, and supper, also atween meals, an' likewise w'en they wakes up doorin' the night.   Cigarettes kills Americans, but them Spaniards, w'ile they don't edzackly git fat on 'em, they lives to werry old ages.   Cos w'y, they gets all dried up like mummies afore they die, an' every one knows that mummies keeps werry well.   Howsumever, that ain't got nothin' to do with this 'ere yarn wot I'm a-tellin' ye.

"Wot I were a-goin' to say are that the admiral, thinkin' as how we wos a-gettin' putty close to the land, sends the flag leftenant to give his compliments to the cap'n and tell him that he'd better look out.   So the cap'n he calls the orderly, and sends him arter the executive ossifer.   W'en he comes the cap'n says to him, says he, 'The admiral says we'd better look out.'   'Werry good, sir,' says the executive ossifer. Then he goes to his orfice an' calls a messenger an' sends him arter the navigator. An' he says to the navigator, says he, 'The cap'n says we'd better look out.' 'Werry good, sir,' says the navigator. An' then the navigator goes down to the ward-room an' calls a messenger an' says to him, says he, 'Go an' tell the ossifer o' the watch that the executive ossifer says we'd better look out.' The messenger goes up to the bridge, where the ossifer o' the watch are a-walkin' up an' down with his hands in his pockets, an' he says to him, says he, 'The navigator says, sir, as how we'd better look out.' So the ossifer o' the watch he calls a bosun's mate, an' says he to him, says he, 'We'd better look out.' 'Aye, aye, sir,' says the bosun's mate. An' that bosun's mate he comes to me, an' he says, 'Come, tumble up to the mast-head, old puddin' head, an' see if you can smell land.' An' so I tumbles up accordin' as how I war told, an' I does the lookin' out.

"At the same time," continued the Old Sailor, shifting his legs, and taking a squint to windward, "the flag leftenant he sends fur the signal ossifer, an' he says to him, says he, 'The admiral says we'd better look out.' 'Werry good, sir,' says the signal ossifer. An' with that he sends for the signal quartermaster, and he says to him, says he, 'The admiral says the fleet 'd better look out. Send up No. 2741' (or somethin' o' that kind). So the signal quartermaster he gets out the flags, an' gets a signal boy to run 'em up to the main yard-arm. Then putty soon

the other ships sent jackies to the mast-heads, an'
there we wos all four on us a-lookin' out."

"And did you really smell the land?" asked
Henry.

"No, I didn't smell nothin' 'ceptin' a werry strong
breeze from the sou'-sou'east wot war a-tryin' werry
hard fur to blow my nose inside out. Howsumever, that ain't got nawthin' to do with this 'ere
yarn wot I'm a-tellin' ye. I stayed up there fur half
an hour afore I seed anythin' to report. Byme-by,
howsumever, I seed a sort o' rumpus in the water a
mile or so off the starboard bow, an' then I seed
there were somethin' a-floating there. So I ups an'
I sings out, 'Wrack ho!' 'W'ere away?' howls the
ossifer on the bridge, an' I told him. He sent a bosun's mate to report it to the cap'n, an' got orders to
alter his course so's to overhaul it. As we drawed a
little nigher to't I seed it wasn't no wrack, so I sings
out:

"'On deck!'

"'What's the matter with you?' asked the ossifer.

"''Taint no wrack at all, sir,' says I to him, says
I, just like that.

"'Well, what is it?' says he to me, kind o' cross
like.

"'It 'pears to be somethin' alive,' says I.

"'Is it a whale?'

"'No, sir, 'tain't no whale. It's a sea-sarpent.'

"The officer called a cadet an' sent him aloft with
one o' them bino-peculiar glasses. That there cadet

looked right skeert arter he'd trained his peepers on the thing.

"'Below there!' he yelled.

"'Aye, aye,' came the answer.

"'It's the sea-sarpent, sure,' he says.

"Then the ossifer o' the watch sent a messinger to tell the cap'n, an' he came on to the bridge hisself. We wos a-gettin' putty close on to the beast now, so the cap'n give orders to load the six-pounder Hotchkiss in the starboard bow, an' take a crack at the animule."

"Were you near enough to see what it looked like?" asked Henry.

"I should say we wos," answered the Old Sailor, "an' it weren't putty to look at. His body, ef you kin say a sarpent has a body, were green an' brown in great big patches, an' it were covered with scales about the size o' dinner plates. These here scales were white on the under side, an' w'en he bent hisself so that the j'ints opened an' the under sides showed he looked for all the world like a werry large-sized demon out o' a fairy play in some theaytre. But his body weren't nawthin' w'en ye came to look at his head, fur that were simply disgustin.' His face were a sort o' salmon-color, jess like one o' them sick-lookin' babboons ye see in cages in Central Park in Noo Yawk, an' he had pink hair parted in the middle. Cos w'y, he were bald-headed on top. He looks at the ship kind o' lazy, an' blinks his eyes; then, jess as they wos a-goin' to plug away at him with the six-pounder, he ups flukes, as the whalers say, an' goes down.

"Howsumever," continued the Old Sailor, after a momentary pause, "he didn't stay down long, but comes up on the other side o' the ship an' blows the water out o' his nose like he were a sparm-whale in his flurry.

"'Now,' says the admiral, 'let him have it.'

"An' the flag leftenant says to the cap'n, an' the cap'n says to the executive ossifer, an' says he to the diwision ossifer in charge o' the six-pounders, an' says the diwision ossifer to the cap'n o' the gun, 'Commence firin'.' An' bang goes the gun. An' bang it goes agin. An' also agin. An' wot d' ye think happened?"

"What?"

"The bloomin' sarpent jess kind o' swayed one side, like a good boxer, an' let the shells go past him. Then he opens his mouth an' he laffs fit to kill hisself."

"Laughed?"

"Yep, that's wot I said. He laffs, an' all on one note, like this:

Ha　ha　ha　ha ha ha　ha ha ha ha!

"An' his voice sounded edzackly like a bugle.

"'Cease firin',' says the admiral.

"An' the flag leftenant tells the cap'n, an' he

tells the executive ossifer, an' he tells the diwision ossifer, an' he says to the captain o' the gun, 'Cease firin'.' So he ceases. An' we all waits to see wot they'd do nex'. Wot d' ye suppose they tried?"

"I'm sure I don't know," said Henry. "I should think they would all have run away; I should."

"Waal, that 'd hardly do, would it? No, they made up their minds they'd try an' catch him. So they had a gang o' seamen rig up a shark line an' bait it with a piece o' nice fresh pork. They hove that over the side, an' waited to see if the sea-sarpent would tackle it. Sure 'nuff, he went down arter that bait an' grabbed it so hard he nigh pulled some o' the hands overboard. The nex' second the line snapped, an' the fishin' party all rolled over one another back'ard. The sarpent came up an' sat up there, grinnin' and chewin' away like he were the most satisfied pusson on 'arth. He were a-havin' a nice fresh pork breakfast, he were, an' it didn't cost him nothin' neither. The men pulled in the line an' found that the bait, an' the hook, too, was gone. One on 'em says he, 'I hope it 'll chuck the bloomin' red-headed sea-monkey to death,' says he, just like that. But it didn't. No, siree. Wot that there sarpent didn't know ain't wuth tellin' about. W'en he gets through chewin' the pork off the hook, he winks both eyes, draws back his head quicker 'n lightnin', an', snappin' it like a whip, he throws the iron hook at the arter bridge, where it catches old Whiskers' cap an' knocks it clean over into the sea."

The Old Sailor now paused to indulge in one of his quiet laughs.

"Mebbe," he continued, presently, "the admiral weren't mad, an' mebbe he were. Leastways, it ain't fur me to go a-criticisin' o' so great a ossifer. Anyhow, he turns kind o' purple around the mouth, an' gives orders to ram the bloomin' reptile. Now, I don't see w'y the sarpent didn't dive, but he didn't seem to be up to them rammin' tactics. So the *Chicago* hits him square in the middle, and cuts him in two."

"And that was the end of him," exclaimed Henry.

"Oh, it were, were it? P'r'aps it's you wot's a-tellin' o' this yarn, an' not me. No, it weren't the end o' him, not by a long sight. Cos w'y, there wos two sarpents now instid o' one."

"What do you mean?"

"Jess wot I says. The hind part o' him sprouted a new head in less'n half a minute, only it had blue hair, an' then the two sarpents sat up on their hunkers an' laffed at us, only now they had two voices, an' they laughed this:

Ha ha   ha   ha ha ha ha ha ha   ha ha ha ha!

The Old Sailor gave a very good imitation of a bugle.

"That's the way it sounded," he said. "Now the

"'HE WINKS BOTH EYES, DRAWS BACK HIS HEAD, AND THROWS THE IRON HOOK AT THE ARTER-BRIDGE'"

admiral got putty well rattled, but he wosn't a-goin'
to give in, so he orders the *Boston* to ram one o' the
new sarpents, an' he'd ram the other with the *Chicago*. They perceeds to do so, an' as any one might
'a' knowed arter wot 'd already happened, they had
four sarpents, with red, white, blue, and green hair,
a-sittin' up and laffin' at 'em. An' now they had
four notes, an' laffed like this:

Ha   ha   ha   ha   ha   ha.

"'Wot call's that?' screamed the admiral.

"'Please, sir,' says the signal ossifer, 'that's the
beginnin' o' a song called "Where did you get that
hat?"'"

"The admiral he orders the ship's engines turned
up to full speed. 'I want to get away from this,'
says he. The signal ossifer whispered somethin' to
him, an' he says, 'Try it.' So the bugler were ordered to sound the church-call over the side at the
sarpents. He blowed it kind o' shaky, but still you
could tell wot it were. Wot do you think happened?"

"What?"

"All four sarpents let out a scream that sounded
like they was bein' cut to pieces, turned up their
tails an' dived straight down. An' that were the
last we ever seed on 'em; but we l'arned w'en we

7

got into port that the sea-sarpent had been seen the werry next day in four different places, hundreds o' miles apart. We never said a word, but we knowed that ef it hadn't been fur old Whiskers, there would never 'a' been four sea-sarpents instid o' one."

It was a hot morning with a flat calm. The sea was as smooth as molasses, and the swells ran in long, slow, oily folds, reflecting the clouds in queer distorted smudges of white and silver. The sails of two or three schooners which were not far off shore hung limp and flapping to and fro, while the creaking of the swaying spars could plainly be heard on shore. Every visible object wavered as the tremulous invisible curtain of radiating heat arose before it. Everything seemed to be overcome with lassitude except a fast steam-yacht, which was ripping the lucent blue into shivering sprays of snow under her black prow as she fled southward, doing a good seventeen knots an hour.

"Aye, aye," muttered the Old Sailor, dangling his legs over the end of the pier, "that's wot's knocked the sport out o' yachtin'. Nobody wants fur to sail now jess fur the fun o' sailin'. They wants to get somew'ere, an' get there soon, an' so they goes an' builds them there iron kettles, an' goes steamin' away, blow fair or blow foul. An' they calls that yachtin'."

Then he laughed one of those peculiar laughs

of his, which seemed to be all on the inside. Presently he put his hand to his brow and said :

"Blow me fur pickles ef I ain't a-sweatin' sittin' still. It's 'most as hot as it were the time Cap'n Jonas Whitby an' me caught the monkey."

"What was that? A monkey, did you say?" It was the voice of Henry Hovey, who, accompanied by his brother George, had stolen up behind the Old Sailor unheard.

"Oh, there ye are!" exclaimed the Old Sailor. "Ain't it hot enough fur ye in the house without comin' out in the sun?"

"Why, we don't mind the heat," said Henry; "besides, we were in swimming a few minutes ago, and now we are perfectly cool."

"And," added George, "we'd like very much to hear about that monkey."

"He were a werry intellectooal monkey, he were," said the Old Sailor, "an' arter I got to know him right well, I were mighty sorry I'd helped to catch him. 'Cos w'y, he caught me."

"Oh, please tell us about him!" exclaimed Henry.

"Don't hurry me," said the Old Sailor. "I ain't so young as I were, an' it takes me more time to git under way."

"But when you do get under way," said Henry, "you can carry a lot of canvas."

"My son, don't try to talk too salt. It don't come nateral to a landsman. Howsumever, I were a-goin'

to tell you about me an' Cap'n Jonas Whitby an'
the monkey. I don't reckon he would 'a' been
edzackly satisfied to be called a monkey, though. I
s'pose he war a sort o' ape, or a orang-otang. Annyhow, he were the biggest, smartest, humanest monkey wot I ever seed, an' he knowed a heap more 'n
lots o' men, an' could learn more 'n twicet as fast.
It were in the year o' '57. Cap'n Jonas Whitby
were master o' the ship *B'iled Rags*. I dunno w'y
she were called that 'ceptin' that it were her name.
I were second-mate, an' a mean, low-down fellow
named Jeroboam Towzle were fust-mate. I ain't
goin' to say nothin' ag'in him now, 'cos w'y, he's
under hatches, an' ye mustn't say nothin' ag'in' a
man w'en he's there. But Towzle were not nice.
Ef he had 'a' bin, mebbe all o' this here yarn wot
I'm a-goin' fur to tell ye wouldn't 'a' took place.
Annyhow, the *B'iled Rags* were bound fur the port
o' Hoodoo, w'ich as everybody knows is in latitood
49° 15' south an' longitood 192° 72' west, w'ich is
no more nor less 'n sayin' that it's on the east coast
o' Africa, about 275 miles north o' You Gander.
The *B'iled Rags* carried a permiskyous cargo, fur
Cap'n Jonas Whitby he allowed that he didn't
know jess edzackly wot the fashions was at Cape
Town, where he laid out fur to call, an' he were
detarmined to have somethin' to please all tastes.

"Waal," continued the Old Sailor, after mopping
the perspiration from his brow with a large red
handkerchief, "there mought 'a' bin many a wuss

v'yage than wot we made in the *B'iled Rags* from
Sandy Hook light-ship to Table Bay. I won't say
as how we didn't git in the doldrums off St. Paul's
Rocks, and I won't deny that w'en we wos about 175
miles nor'west o' the bay we fell in with the gale o'
wind w'ich stopped the *Flyin' Dutchman*, an' it
blowed us clean away down into the latitood where
they don't have no summer 'ceptin' in the almanac.
Howsumever, arter bein' hove to fur a week with
the seas runnin' ninety feet high, accordin' to my
carkilations, an' rollin' our yard-arms under, we got
a fair wind, an' clappin' on all stuns'ls we squeezed
the old hooker up to thirteen knots an hour, an'
climbed back into the civilized part o' the ocean.
We made good tradin' in Table Bay, an' Cap'n Jonas
Whitby, who were the chief owner o' the *B'iled
Rags*, says he to me, says he, 'I'll git a pianny fur
my wife an' a boardin'-school eddication fur my
darter out o' this 'ere same v'yage,' says he to me.
An' says I to him, 'Werry good, too, sir,' says I to
him, jess like that, bein' second-mate o' the ship an'
more used to workin' than talkin'.

   " From Cape Town we went right up to Hoodoo,
it bein' our puppose there to trade with the natives
fur elephants' tusks. Now Hoodoo are about two
miles back from the sea, but there are a werry fair
harbor on the coast. We laid there at anchor fur
about two weeks, doorin' w'ich time we wos a-gettin'
the remains o' our cargo ashore an' the ivory aboard.
One mornin', jess before we wos ready to set sail,

I seed a large an' han'some monkey a-walkin' up an' down the beach near the edge o' the forest. He war a-scratchin' his head once in a w'ile, an' lookin' kind o' puzzled, like a man wot had found hisself onexpectedly in a noo place. I p'inted him out to Cap'n Jonas Whitby, an' says he to me, says he, 'I'm a-goin' fur to capture that there monk an' take him back to Noo Yawk, w'ere I'll get a werry good price fur him.' An' says I to him, says I, 'Cap'n Jonas Whitby, I wouldn't have nothin' to do with a monk like that wot looks as if he knowed more 'n a respectable sailor-man,' says I. But Cap'n Jonas Whitby he laughed, an' ordered a boat got ready fur to take him ashore. He were a werry particular man, were Cap'n Jonas Whitby, an' ef he wanted a monkey, he'd jess got to have one.

"Waal, he tuk a lasso with him fur to throw over the monkey's head when he'd sneak up close enough. I were a-watchin' him all the time, an' blow me fur pickles ef I don't think the monk were too. Annyhow, w'en the Cap'n finally got around behind the beast an' threw the lasso over his head, the bloomin' monk didn't try to get away at all. No, sir; on the contrairy, he werry dignifiedlike walked along the beach to where the boat were, stepped in, an' sat down in the starn-sheets werry much as ef he were a actin' rear-admiral. Cap'n Jonas Whitby walked along behind, and seemed to think it war the werry finest joke wot he'd ever met with. He came off with the monk in the boat, brought him

aboard the *B'iled Rags*, walked him up to me, an'
says he, 'Let me interjuce you to Admiral Hoodoo.'
That's what he called the monk, jess like that, he
bein' Cap'n o' the ship.　The monk, he never says a
word ; 'cos w'y, bein' a monkey, how could he ?
But I didn't like the way he looked out o' his eye.
Howsumever, I didn't say nothin', fur I knowed
that Cap'n Jonas Whitby would jess laugh at me.
The monk behaved hisself so well that he was allowed to go around the ship putty much as he liked,
all hands watchin' to see that he didn't get into any
boat wot were goin' ashore.　The monk didn't seem
to want to get away.　He went all over the ship,
though, an' he examined everything as ef he wos a
human bein' chuck-full o' curiosity.　He even went
into the chart-room an' pulled down the charts an'
looked 'em all over werry solemnlike.　I thought
that were funny then, but arterwards I didn't."

　　" Why didn't you afterwards ?" asked George.

　　" That are wot I are a-comin' to in the course o'
this 'ere yarn wot I'm a-tellin' you," gravely responded the Old Sailor.　He again mopped the perspiration from his brow and proceeded.　" Byme-by
we hove up the mud-hook, an' got under way fur
home.　We had all the ivory we wanted, an' one
monk wot I didn't think we did want.　I were
mighty sure that monk were a Jonah."

　　" What is a Jonah ?" asked Henry.

　　" A Jonah are what a sailor-man calls any person
wot he thinks makes bad luck fur the ship.　Fur

three days we had the finest kind o' weather an' fair winds. That were because the bloomin' monk were sea-sick. On the fourth day the monk got well an' went an' sat down on the poop alongside o' the man at the wheel. He hadn't been there ten minutes w'en the bosun comes aft an' reports that two o' the men in the fo'k'sle was werry sick, an' he'd like werry much ef one o' the mates would come an' take a look at 'em. I went, an' had to come back an' tell the cap'n that I thought they had a fever o' some sort. An', sure 'nuff, they had. Inside o' twenty-four hours them men wos ravin' lunatics, an' four more wos took down. Then it come on to blow from the sou'west. Bein' short-handed, we couldn't get the *B'iled Rags* down to short canvas as soon as we ought to, an' the result were that her mizzen-to'gallant mast were carried away, an' five men wos knocked overboard an lost. All this time that bloomin' monk seemed quite easy in his mind. He jess walked around the ship, a-hangin' on to ropes with them big paws, an' examinin' things keerfully wherever he went.

"Waal, to make the story short, when that gale were over, between men lost overboard an' disabled, an' others laid up with the fever, there were nobody left to handle the ship 'ceptin' Cap'n Jonas Whitby an' me. The cap'n he says to me, says he, 'Wot d' ye think we'd better do?' That's wot he says. An' says I to him, says I, 'I guess we got to make fur the nearest port we kin with the wind aft.'

Jess as I said that I turned my head, an' there were the monk standin' right behind us an' listenin' to every word we said. And wot d' ye think happened then?"

"What?" exclaimed both boys.

"The monk picks up a belayin'-pin an' drives the cap'n an' me away from the wheel, wich the same he tuk hold o' hisself, an' beginned fur to steer the ship, jess like that, him bein' a brown monkey an' we bein' two sailor - men. An' the bloomin' monk he puts the ship on a nor'westerly course, an' sits there a-lookin' puffickly satisfied with the entire perceedin's. Cap'n Jonas Whitby he looked at me an' I looked at him, an' then we went below to get the cap'n's pistols. But, bless ye! the monk were jess as smart as we wos. As soon as we'd opened the chest an' got out the pistols, an' afore we could load 'em, there were the monk right alongside o' us, an' he grabbed the pistols out o' the cap'n's hands, an' throwed 'em through a port into the sea. Then he up an' cuffed each o' us alongside o' the jaw an' shuk his head, as much as to say that we mustn' try any monkey business with him, 'cos why, he were in that business hisself.

"Then," continued the Old Sailor, after wiping away the perspiration once more, "the monk ordered us on deck, an' we had to go. Once there he tuk the wheel agin. The wind were dead astern, an' I knowed that ef we kep' on sailin' on that course we'd get back putty near to where we started from.

"'AN' THE BLOOMIN' MONK SAT THERE A LOOKIN' SATISFIED.'"

Now that monkey seemed to know that jess as well as we did. Fust thing I knowed he were makin' motions at us, an' at the main-tops'l, which were reefed. We suspected wot he wanted, an' pertended not to onderstan'. Then he comes down off the poop with a jump, an' begins to club us with a belayin'-pin, jess like he were a fust-mate an' we two onwillin' sailors. So we had to go aloft an' get the reefs out o' that sail, w'ich the same it are no easy job fur two pussons. But the monk kep' us puttin' more canvas on her all day, an' by night she war bowlin' along at about nine knots an hour. The monk made us git our supper an' his too. Then he put Cap'n Jonas Whitby at the wheel, an' began to look round fur a place to sleep. Suddenly he seemed to have a noo idea. He tuk his belayin'-pin between his teeth, jumped into the mizzen riggin', ran up to the mizzen-top, an' curled up there. You see, he could tell the minute we changed the course o' the ship.

"Arter that display o' jedgment, Cap'n Jonas Whitby and me we jess give right in, an' let the monk have his own way. 'Cos w'y, wot could we do with all the men that were aboard a-layin' below with a fever? Even ef we had got the ship on another course we wasn't strong enough to haul the yards around so as to trim the sails proper. So, to bring this here yarn wot I'm a-tellin' ye more towards its nateral end, I'll jess say that Cap'n Jonas Whitby an' me sailed that there blessed old

hooker the *B'iled Rags* under the orders o' a long-
legged orang-otang for three days, and then we
sighted land. We managed to get word down to
the men forward o' wot were goin' on, but they was
too sick to help us. The land proved to be a p'int
on the coast about two miles below Hoodoo. The
monk helped us to let go the anchor an' git a boat
lowered, an' he were as strong as five men, he were.
Then he made us row him ashore. W'en we got
there he made us get out o' the boat, an' march
ahead o' him fur about a mile back into the forest,
an' there we walked right into a reg'lar village o'
monkeys livin' in thatched huts. W'en they seed
him they set up a mos' drefful squealin'. He pointed at us, an' they squealed more. We made up our
minds that our time had come, but we soon learned
that they didn't want to kill us. They wanted to
keep us fur slaves, an' make us work fur them.
Lucky, though, w'en we came ashore we brought a
gallon demijohn full o' hard cider. W'en we wos
shut up in a hut fur the night, we put the demijohn
outside, an' the monkeys got it. O' course they'd
never had annythin' stronger 'n cocoanut milk before, an' it went to their heads. So they all fell
asleep, an' slept like they wos dead.

"Then Cap'n Jonas Whitby an' me we riz up, an'
climbed out through a hole in the thatched roof o'
our hut, an' run. We run the whole way down to
the beach, jumped into the boat, an' rowed off to
the ship. Early in the mornin' we found that half

a dozen o' the sick men was well enough to help us git up the anchor, an' we started at it. But, bless you, the monks wasn't through with us yit."

"What did they do?" asked Henry.

"They come down to the beach by hundreds, each one carryin' two or three cocoanuts, an' screechin' terrible. W'en they seed how fur the ship were from the shore, they got hold o' young saplin's, bent 'em down to the ground, stuck cocoanuts on the top branches, an' let go. My lands! The way them saplin's fired them cocoanuts at us were most terrifyin'. We worked hard an' got the anchor, an', as good luck would have it, the wind were off shore, an' we soon got out o' reach. An' so Cap'n Jonas Whitby an' me an' the sailors an' the *B'iled Rags* all got back to America agin. But what d' ye s'pose Cap'n Jonas Whitby does now w'en he sees a orang-otang?"

"What?" asked the boys.

"He jess picks up his heels an' runs away," said the Old Sailor, gravely. "'Cos w'y, Cap'n Jonas Whitby ain't a-takin' no more chances on monks."

T was a hard winter day—
one of those days when the
horizon seems to have been
cut out of cold steel and
thrust up against the sky
just to make the clouds look far, far away. The Old
Sailor walked briskly out on the pier, catching the
nails on the soles of his shoes with sturdy digs into
the little ovals of ice that gleamed here and there
where the salt spray had whirled through the biting
air and frozen almost as soon as it touched the planks.
The two boys spied their old friend as he beat to

windward from the outer end of the pier, and with glad shouts ran to meet him.

"Come up to the house," called Henry; "you must be half frozen."

"Waal," answered the Old Sailor, with a quizzical smile, "I ain't edzackly wot ye might call half frozen, nor I ain't parb'iled nuther. It are right properly cool this 'ere day, an' I don't mind ef I do drink some more o' your mother's b'ilin' hot coffee, w'ich the same it are o' the werry finest."

The three friends walked briskly to the house, and the Old Sailor, having divested himself of a huge "comforter," which went round and round his neck, for all the world, as he described it, like a "gasket around a Irishman's reef," sat down and warmed his heart with the ready coffee.

"Now," he said, peering through the window at the hard blue sea, "look at that 'ere barky out there a-staggerin' along under her royals in this 'ere breeze o' wind w'en she might jess as well be under to'gallants an' doin' as many knots an' a-savin' her masts. But, bless you! some cap'ns 'ain't got no sort o' hearts fur their blessed ships. Now there were old Silas Mackleboy, wot were cap'n o' the ship *Mock Turtle*, w'ich the same I were fust-mate, w'en she ran afoul o' the Boyking Islands. An' by the same token that were one o' the werry partick- lerly piculiar carcumstances o' my voyidges."

"The Boyking Islands!" exclaimed Henry; "why, they're not in my geography."

"No, nor nobody's else's," said the Old Sailor; "they ain't on no chart; an' I don't more'n half b'lieve there is any sich place, 'ceptin' that I bin there an' seed 'em."

"Where did you see them?"

"Waal, that are the werry yarn wot I'm a-goin' fur to tell ye."

The Old Sailor tossed off the last dregs of the coffee, wiped his mouth, cast a quick glance at the staggering bark, settled himself back in the chair, and began thus:

"Waal, may I never scuttle a lobster-pot agin ef this 'ere weren't the werry way it happened. It were in the year 1859, an' we sot sail from Bosting with a mixed cargo o' beans an' perlite literatoor fur distribution among the ignorant savidges o' Patagonia. It were a scheme o' some Bosting ladies fur eddikatin' of 'em up to the p'int o' wearin' shirts along with their collars. Howsumever, that 'ain't got nothin' to do with this 'ere yarn wot I'm a-tellin' ye. Cap'n Silas, he sez to me, sez he, 'The sooner we gets down there an' discharges this 'ere cargo o' heavy feedin' an' readin',' the sooner I'll feel safe aboard o' my own ship.' So wot does he do but he cracks on sail till I jess about reckoned that ef it blowed any harder the bloomin' old hooker 'd open up all her seams an' let the beans right out into Davy Jones's locker. We wos a-smotherin' an' a-smokin' through it all the time fur the fust week, an' in the night watches I used to think I could jess fairly see the Southern Cross a-climbin' up behind the sea, an' gittin' ready fur to come into sight with a hop, skip, an' a jump, like a circus clown a-hollerin' 'Here we is agin.' Waal, sure 'nuff, we run ca-smack into the doldrums.

"This 'ere sort o' thing went on fur six days. Oncet in a while a little puff 'd come along an' jess put steerage-way on her, but practically she only kind o' washed along with the surface current. Waal, Cap'n Silas were 'most crazy, w'en, all on a suddent, one o' the hands wot was doin' a odd job aloft sings out, 'Land ho !' Nobody said a word fur a minute, 'cos w'y, we was right down on to the hequator, an' there weren't no land near us, accordin' to the chart, nearer 'n St. Paul's Rocks, w'ich the same wos about five hundred miles east o' us. Cap'n Silas axed the man w'ere the land were, an' he said as how it were right ahead o' us. Then Cap'n Silas allowed as how he wos about to make a discovery o' a new island, an' he sez to me, sez he, ' I'm a-goin' fur to explore this 'ere land an' find out what it are.'

"Waal, blow me fur pickles ef 'twarn't two days afore we got to the bloomin' island, an' then we sees there was two on 'em, with a small channel atween 'em. We was a-wonderin' whether we couldn't make a anchorage in the mouth of this channel w'en we seed a boat a-puttin' orf from the shore. Cap'n Silas had arms sarved out, 'cos w'y, we didn't know but the natyves might be fond o' eatin' sailor-men. But putty soon the boat came within hailin' distance,

8

an' then we seed that it were manned by middle-aged an' old men, an' a boy o' ten were in command. An' sez I to myself, sez I, 'I wonder ef these 'ere blessed islands is settled by a few ships' companies of the United States navy?' sez I. The boy he signified that his designs wos ontirely peacific, an' he were allowed to come aboard. As soon as he seed Cap'n Silas, he walked up to him, and sez he to him, sez he, 'His Majesty King Bucky the Seckind would be werry pleased to have you wisit him at his castle, an' he'd like to know ef there's anything wot ye wants.'

"An' the cap'n he ups an' sez he, 'I wouldn't mind fillin' my water-tanks.' An' the boy sez to him, sez he, 'Fetch your ship to anchor in the channel yonder ; there's ten fathoms there, an' ye'll find a well about a quarter o' a mile to the south'ard. You needn't be afraid o' landin' men. Nobody 'll not do ye no harm here. We is peaceable kids, an' all we axes is to be let alone.'

"Waal, the long an' short o' the whole business were that most o' us went ashore, me a-goin' with the cap'n to wisit his majesty. We was putty much puzzled afore we got there, 'cos w'y : everywhere we seed old people workin', an' boys bossin' 'em. W'y, we stopped stock-still in front o' one house hearing a twelve-year-old boy sayin', 'Now, mother, get up out o' that an' peel the potaters ; an', father, it's five minutes arter nine, an' you 'ain't bin down to buy my mornin' candy yet. Come, now, jump,

or I'll send you to bed without any supper to-night.'
Cap'n Silas, sez he to me, sez he, 'I'd like to give that
boy a sound spankin'.' An' our escort, a boy o' ten,
sez he, 'You'd better not let the king hear any such
talk, or he'll have you spanked.' 'Me spanked?'
sez Cap'n Silas. 'Yes,' sez the boy. 'Only grown-
up folks gets spanked in the Boyking Islands, an'
we makes 'em holler, too, an' promise never to do it
agin.'

"Waal, we wondered more an' more wot kind o'
a place we'd got into, but we didn't say nothin'
more, but waited to see the king.   Bless your heart !
W'en at last we wos brought into his majesty's
presence, he were a boy o' twelve !   'How d' ye do?'
sez he, 'an' w'ere d' ye come from ; and is grown-up
people still bosses in America?'   Then he went on
to explain the whole business.   The Boyking Islands
wos islands w'ere a boy were allus king, an' w'ere
boys wos the bosses, an' old folks had to mind 'em.
'Yes,' sez King Bucky the Seckind, 'we boys got
tired o' bein' down-trodden by our fathers an' mothers an' uncles an' aunts, so we riz up an' took pos-
session o' the governmint, an' fur sixty year we bin
a-runnin' things our own way.   The king are elected
out o' the boys seven year old, an' he reigns till he
are fifteen.   Then he takes the position o' chief o'
police, an' holds that till he are twenty - one, arter
w'ich age all pussons retire from the public service
here.   As soon as a man gits married he has to go to
work fur the governmint, w'ich allows him so much

land an' a house. As soon as there is a boy born in
the family, the father an' mother does all their work
fur him, and gives the governmint six per cent. fur
taxes.'

"'How 'bout gals?' sez Cap'n Silas.

"'Oh, gals ain't no good!' sez King Bucky the
Seckind, jess like any other boy o' twelve. 'The
police seems to like 'em, an' they is good fur cookin'
an' mendin' an' bein' people's mothers and sich
things; but they don't count in these here islands.
But they has a putty good time, 'cos bein' let alone
they does putty much ez they pleases. They'd look
better, though, ef they had teeth.'

"'W'y, 'ain't they got no teeth?' sez Cap'n
Silas.

"'No,' sez the king; 'their teeth allus turns black
an' falls out. The old people sez it's 'cos they eats
so much candy; but wot grown-up folks sez don't
go here.'

"'But I should think,' sez I, 'that the dentists
would—'

"'Dentists!' sez the king; 'you let me catch a
dentist anywhere on these 'ere islands! Dentists is
shot on sight, my friend.'

"'But you has doctors, don't ye?"

"'Yep,' sez he; 'we has to have 'em fur stomach-
aches, w'ich the same rages werry bad in these islands at all seasons o' the year. But all the doctors
has to be homœopathics; an' we don't allow no
lancin', nor blisterin', nor sich things.'

"'STOMACH-ACHES,' W'ICH THE SAME RAGES WERRY BAD AT ALL SEASONS OV THE YEAR'"

"'Wot are the principal manufacture o' these islands o' yourn?' sez Cap'n Silas.

"'Candy,' sez King Bucky the Seckind.

"'Do you export much?'

"'Not a stick. We eats it all ourselves. But you must come an' see the royal candy factories afore you go. They are run by the governmint, an' are directed by the princes o' the royal blood.'

"'Then I s'pose candy's putty high-priced?'

"'Oh no,' sez the king; 'candy's werry reasonable. The price is fixed by law, ye see. O' course, it wouldn't do to let it be dear, 'cos w'y, that 'd make the governmint onpopular, an' then there'd be plots to try an' git the king out o' power. O' course, sometimes the people does git a little restless, but we allus fixes that.'

"'How?' sez I to him, sez I.

"'W'y, the royal family gives a circus.'

"'Oh, do you keep a circus?'

"'Keep one? No; we *is* one. See here.'

"An' the king he got down off the throne, an' did a row o' back hand-springs, windin' up with a twistin' somerset. I tell you he were jess great at it.

"'There,' sez he to me, sez he; 'any feller wot can't do that with all his clothes on 'ain't got no show to be elected king o' the Boyking Islands.'

"'I bin a-thinkin',' sez Cap'n Silas to him, 'that you can't live on candy. Don't ye have somethin' else to eat?'

"'Oh yes,' sez the king ; 'there's cake an' pie an' plum-puddin', an' several other sich things as them.'

"'Don't ye make any bread ?' sez I.

"'Sure,' sez the king ; 'lots o' that. Fathers an' mothers ain't allowed to have no cake, nor candy, nor pie, except at Christmas. They has to eat bread an' b'iled pertaters an' fried fish an' things. Sometimes they gits into the pantry an' steals cake an' jam, an' gits spanked an' sent to bed early.'

"'How early ?'

"'Six o'clock. Their reg'lar bedtime are eight. No grown-up folks is allowed to sit up arter that, 'cos they has to git up an' go to school.'

"'Oh, does they go to school ?'

"'O' course. Does ye think we're a lot o' igno-ramuses here ? Everybody has to go to school wot's passed the age o' twenty-one.'

"'How many years do they go ?'

"'Twenty years. Most on 'em don't live much longer than that. Say, you want to understand that we've got things fixed jess right here fur boys.'

"'Are the grown-up folks allowed to vote ?' sez the cap'n, as if that idee jess struck him.

"'No, siree!' sez the king. 'W'y, they'd be a-tryin' to upset the governmint. Nobody kin vote wot's passed the age o' twenty-one.'

"'But,' sez I to him, sez I, 'I don't see jess how you keep 'em under. They're bigger 'n' stronger.'

"'Waal,' sez the king to me, sez he, 'there's twicet as many o' us as there is o' them, an' then most o'

"'EVERYBODY HAS TO GO TO SCHOOL WOT'S PASSED THE AGE O' TWENTY-ONE.'"

them has sich poor digestions that they ain't werry good fur much at all. Sometimes their children brings 'em to the circus jess to try an' cheer 'em up a bit, but it don't seem to. Grown-up folks ain't much good, anyhow. Boys is better. Even gals is better.'

"Waal, you may be sure that Cap'n Silas 'n' me was doin' a good deal o' thinkin'. It seemed like a downright shame to us that all them fathers an' mothers was a-workin', an' the kids havin' all the fun, an' at the same time a-ruinin' their innards with candy an' pie an' sich. I said somethin' o' the sort to the king, an' he laffed.

"'Oh yes,' sez he; 'I know wot you think. You ain't the fust strangers as 'a' bin here. But ain't it all square? Byme-by I'll get too old to be king, an' I'll git to be growed up an' married, an' my boy 'll come along an' have all the fun I bin a-havin'. An' he'll have his fun w'en he's a boy, an' fun *is* fun; not w'en he's a head o' a family an' ain't got no time to have fun, an' are too old to turn hand-springs or play football. This 'ere kingdom are run accordin' to common-sense, an' all the other countries in the world is dead wrong. We knows our business, we boys does; an' we means fur to go it while we're young, 'cos w'en we gits old we can't.'

"Waal, nothin' pertikler occurrin' to Cap'n Silas or me, we kep' our mouths shet. But jess the same it didn't seem edzackly a square deal on the old folks. So that night, w'en we wos aboard the ship agin, we talked it all over, an' detarmined that

somethin' ort to be did fur to rouse up the grown-
up folks on them islands to strike fur liberty. Cap'n
Silas sez he to me, sez he, 'I'll go ashore in the
mornin', an' talk to the old man who lives down by
the well w'ere we gits our water.' An' me bein' mate
an' him cap'n, I couldn't say nothin' 'ceptin' ' All
right,' w'ich the same I said, jess like that. The
next mornin', sure 'nuff, the cap'n did go an' have
a talk with the old man, but he come back in about
half an hour a-shakin' his head. 'It ain't no sort o'
good,' sez he to me, sez he ; ' the old man says that
the boys kin lick their fathers every time. The fact
o' the matter is that, so far as I kin see, by the time
these people git growed up their innards is so de-
structified with eatin' candy an' cake an' pie an' sich
truck that they 'ain't got no strength nor no courage.'

"Waal, that weren't the end o' 't. About an hour
later a company o' boy sodjers, headed by a drummer
playin' on a toy drum an' a ossifer carryin' a tin
sword, an' they themselves a-carryin' little wooden
guns with tin bar'ls, come a-marchin' down to the
shore. The ossifer he salutes, an' sez he to Cap'n
Silas, sez he, 'The king wants to see you.' So off
went the cap'n. In an hour he come back, an' he
were a-laffin' 'most fit to bust hisself. 'Wot d' ye
think ?' sez he to me, sez he. ' I don't think nothin'
till you tells me wot to think,' sez I to him, sez I, me
bein' mate o' the ship an' him cap'n. 'Waal,' sez
he, 'some one's bin an' told King Bucky the Seckind
that I bin a-talkin' treason to the old man, an' his

majesty's give us three hours to quit the islands.'
'Then,' sez I, 'we'd better stand by to slip our
cable.' 'Not much!' sez he, 'but I guess we'll
heave short an' be ready to git under way quick.
There's no tellin' wot he'll do.' Waal, sure 'nuff,
we didn't go at the time we wos ordered to, an' putty soon we heerd a tremenjous beatin' o' toy drums
an' blowin' o' toy trumpets. Down comes the king
at the head o' his army o' boys—six hundred o' 'em,
there was—an' they opened fire on us."

"With what?" asked Henry.

"With toy cannons loaded with gravel by way o'
grape-shot; with bow-guns firin' bolts wot had pins
stickin' out o' the ends; with blow-pipes an' bean-
shooters an' sling-shots. Say, ef ever you git under
fire o' three hundred bean - shooters at onect you'll
wish you'd never bin born. Cap'n Silas danced an'
hollered, an' the sailors danced an' hollered, an'
couldn't man the capstan - bars. So I slipped the
cable, an' let the old hooker drift out o' the channel
starn fust. An' we made sail on to her, an' got out o'
that country jess as quick as ever we knowed how."

"And you've never been back?"

"That are the queer part o' 't. I tried to go back
onect, an' made the latitood an' longitood right; but
the islands wasn't there; an' no one's ever bin able
fur to find 'em sence."

And the Old Sailor looked so solemn and mys-
terious that the boys did not dare to ask any more
questions.

"YES, there he is," said Henry.

The boys had gone down to the pier to look for the Old Sailor. It was Saturday, and as there was no school they were in hopes that their old friend would tell them a yarn. He was sitting in his favorite place at the end of the pier, gazing out on the ocean. The boys followed the direction of his gaze, and saw a two-masted schooner-rigged steamer, deeply laden, ploughing her way southward at a slow pace, with an acre of foam rising almost to her hawse-pipes. She rolled slowly and heavily as she went, and poured an oily column of black smoke from her single fat funnel.

" An' wot kind o' a wessel do ye think that are ?" asked the Old Sailor, without looking around.

" A steamer, of course," said Henry.

" An' werry good, too, so fur as it goes," responded the Old Sailor, indulging in one of his silent laughs. "But wot kind o' a steamer ?"

" Looks like a tramp," answered George.

" That's werry good indeed," said the Old Sailor. "A tramp she are an' a tramp she'll be. An' she are werry much like another tramp wot I once knowed, only she are summat shorter an' consid'able more by the head, w'ich the same tramps often is."

" Will you tell us about the tramp you knew ?" asked Henry.

" That are the werry identical thing wot I'm a-standin' by fur to do," said the Old Sailor. He took another careful look at the steamer, and then broke out thus : " W'ich the same ye may call me a marine ef it warn't in the year afore I quit the sea an' come here to spend the rest o' my nateral-born days a-tellin' you boys about it. I shipped as second-mate on to the tramp steamer *Iron Mary*, with a cargo o' tin cans, goat-skins, an' rattlesnakes' teeth fur White's Island."

" Why, what are rattlesnakes' teeth good for ?" asked George.

" The natyves o' that island," answered the Old Sailor, " wear them an' tin cans fur ornaments, an' goat-skins fur clothes, an' we wos to exchange our cargo fur White's Island oats, w'ich the same will make a slow hoss fast, only they is werry hard to get, 'cos w'y, the natyves won't trade 'em 'ceptin' in leap-year, it bein' their belief that oats growed in them years ain't good. We got under way from Noo Yawk on a werry fine mornin' in February, an' passin' the Scotland Light-ship at four bells in the forenoon watch, laid our course south by east. The *Iron Mary* were not a werry fast ship, but she were a werry pertiklerly fine-built wessel. She war built in nine water-tight compartments, with slidin' bulk-head doors, so that if she got into a collidgion you could shet up the compartment wot were busted an' keep the water from goin' into any other part. Leastways, that's wot ye could do ef the doors worked all right, w'ich the same they ginerally don't. An' that were the cause o' this 'ere yarn wot I'm a-tellin' ye.

"We had good weather fur several days, an' got about fifteen hundred mile on our course. Then the byrometer beginned fur to go down slow and stiddy. It kep' a-goin' down fur nigh on to two days, an' still the weather were clear an' comf'table. But our old man, Cap'n Waterbury Boggs, sez he to me, sez he, 'Ye know wot the poet sez, don't ye?' An' I allowed I didn't know no poets. An' sez he to me, sez he, 'The poet sez, "Long foretold, long last; short notice, soon past."' An' sez I to him, sez I, 'The poet wot said that were a seafarin' pusson,' jess like that sez I to him, sez I, him bein' the cap'n o' the ship, an' me the second-mate. I hadn't much more'n

got the words out o' my mouth w'en it beginned fur
to cloud up, an' a awful swell rolled up out o' the
southeast. The *Iron Mary* she rolled so that ye
couldn't keep your feet, an' the skipper he changed
her course, so's she'd head into it. At three bells in
the evenin' it beginned fur to blow, an' by midnight
it were a howlin' gale. Afore mornin' it got up to
a hurricane, an' the steamer were a-shippin' water
till I thort her decks 'd be clean stove in. The
cap'n he ordered us to put ile in the drain-pipes,
an' so we soon stopped the breakin' o' the seas, an'
rode better, only the pitchin' were somethin' simply
ridikalous.

"We lay to with the ingin' jess a-turnin' over all
that day, an' as it didn't let up a single bit we made
ready fur another rough night. Toward sundown,
to make things wuss, a measly drivin' mist set in,
an' you couldn't see the end o' your own nose, no
matter how cross-eyed ye looked. The mist lasted
all night, an' were there w'en I turned out to take
the forenoon watch the next day. I hadn't much
more'n got on deck w'en I were shook up by a loud
shout from forrard. I jumped out on the fo'c'sle-
deck, an' one o' the hands yelled : 'A waterlogged
wreck! Driftin' right on to us!' It were a capsized
schooner, an' afore it were possible fur us to do anythin' at all it came tumblin' down the side o' a roarin' mountain o' water jess as we plunged down off
another. Crash! Our forefoot came down on top
o' the wreck. I heerd a great scrapin' an' bangin'

as the schooner drifted out from under us, an' the next second some men come tumblin' up the fore-hatch, cryin': 'The water! It's a-comin' in by the ton!' 'Close the bulkhead doors in the forrard bulkhead!' I yelled. The hands jumped below, an' in a minnit comes back an' sez, 'They're fouled, an' won't shet.' 'Close 'em in the second bulkhead!' I hollered. 'It's done!' they sez. By this time the cap'n were on deck, an' ordered all the boats cleared ready fur lowerin'. 'No boat 'll live in that sea, sir,' sez Isaac Hooper, the fust-mate. 'No more it will,' sez the cap'n. 'So we must try to keep the steamer afloat till the gale moderates. I'll go b'low myself an' see how things is a-goin'.' The cap'n went b'low, an' the rest o' us stood an' looked at each other. All on a suddent Isaac Hooper, the fust-mate, he looks werry piculiar at me, an' sez he to me, sez he,

"'It are my opinion that this 'ere wessel are a-settlin' by the head.'

"'W'ich the same,' sez I to him, sez I, 'is also the opinion o' yourn truly.'

"The next minnit the cap'n comes a-runnin' on deck, an' sez he to me, sez he :

"'We're a-goner. The water are ten foot deep in the forrard compartment, an' are almost the same in the second. She'll go down head-fust in about ten minnits.'

"'I don't b'lieve she'll sink at all,' sez Isaac Hooper to him, sez he.

" ' Wot fur won't she ?' sez the cap'n.

" ' 'Cos them two compartments won't hold 'nuff water fur to drag her down.'

" 'But they'll hold 'nuff fur to pull her head under, an' then these 'ere seas a-breakin' on to her 'll send her down,' sez I to him, sez I.

" Howsumever, 'tain't no use o' tellin' ye wot we all said, 'cos w'y, none on us didn't know nothin' about wot were a-goin' fur to happen. An' how could we, seein' that nothin' o' the sort ever happened afore, an' ain't werry exceedin' likely fur to happen agin."

" What did happen?" asked Henry, eagerly.

"Jess you hold your breath," said the Old Sailor, "an' I'll tell you. The steamer's head kep' a-settlin' an' a-settlin' till all on a sudden her starn riz out o' water, an' the screw whizzed around in the air like a buzz-saw. The deck were now a-slantin' from starn to stem so that ye couldn't stand up on to it, an' all hands was a-hangin' on to the riggin' or life-lines, and putty nigh skeert to death. Now the ingineer an' all his hands come on deck.

" 'Cap'n,' sez the ingineer, ' the screw are up in the air, an' we can't stand up b'low, an' we ain't no more pertik'ler good nohow, so, ef you please, we'd like a chance fur our lives.'

" 'Help yourselves,' sez the cap'n, werry sour-caustic.

" The ingineer he looks around, an' he sees right away that ye couldn't 'a' lowered a boat nohow, 'cos w'y, the way we was a-ridin' they was all jammed ag'n' the forrard davies. All the time the ship's head were a-settlin' more an' more, an' the slant o' the deck were a-gettin' steeper an' steeper. The steamer she swung round so that her starn were facin' the seas, an' that settled it."

The Old Sailor paused for a moment, and while the boys were regarding him with breathless interest he indulged in a silent laugh, after which he continued thus:

"Blow me fur pickles ef 'tain't puffickly silly w'en I comes fur to think on 't now. Wot d' ye think happened?"

"What?" cried both boys.

"W'y, a tremenjous sea rolled up under her starn, heavin' it so high into the air that the *Iron Mary* jess stood on her head. An' there she stopped. We all looked at each other, but no one opened a mouth till the cap'n said,

"'Waal, we can't hang on here in this fashion, so let's all go b'low an' consider wot are to be did.'

"So we climbed up to the cabin companion-way an' fell down into the cabin, where we fetched up on the forrard bulkhead among a permiskyous pile o' furniture an' things. The cap'n he looks into his state-room, an' sez he, werry solemnlike,

"'I got to l'arn to sleep standin' up, I reckon.'

"'Waal,' sez Bill Martin, an able seaman, 'I got to l'arn to sleep under water ef I go to my bunk tonight.'

"The cap'n he laffed, an' sez he to me, sez he, 'I'm a-thinkin' this 'ere gale 'll break afore to-mor-rer, an' then we got to see what kin be did.'

"'We kin git some o' them boats away in quiet weather,' sez Isaac Hooper.

"'I think we kin do better nor that,' sez the cap'n; 'ef we kin find some way to stop up the hole in the bow.'

"'I think it kin be managed,' sez I to him, sez I. 'There are a diver's outfit aboard, an' as I've had some experience in that kind o' work, suppose I go down an' take a look at the hole.'

"'Bully!' sez the cap'n.

"'You'll have to go down on the outside,' sez Isaac Hooper, ''cos w'y, ef ye go down to open the doors to let you down inside the water 'll come through an' the ship 'll sink.'

"So it were decided that as soon as the weather got still I should make the trip. It beginned fur to moderate that night, an' the nex' day the ingi-neer went to work to rig the air-pump to keep me in breath. Waal, it were simply dreadful a-tryin' to do anythin' aboard a ship wot were standin' on her head, an' dancin' slowly up an' down over the swells. But arter a good deal o' hard work an' a awful sight o' talk, the ingineer got the pump set up on a bulkhead. Meantime the crew lowered Bill Martin an' me into the after-hold, w'ere the divin' rig were. Waal, ye never see such a tangle o' things in the whole course o' your life. There wos tin cans, rattlesnakes' teeth,

9

goat-skins, ropes, old iron, boxes, bags, blocks, an' all sorts o' riffraff piled up in the worst kind o' confusion wot ever was knowed sence the destruction o' Sodom an' Tomorrah.

"Howsumever, Bill an' me managed to find the divin' rig, an' to git back into the cabin with 't. The followin' day the sea were quite calm, an' the long easy swells didn't interfere none with our plan. The pumps wos started, an' I climbed out o' the main hatch, w'ich were jess out o' water, an', shet up in the divin' suit, I felt my way forrard—or ruther down'ard—to the ship's bow. I climbed over, an' worked my way around underneath till I got to the hole. It were about five feet in diameter an' putty near round. I shook my head, an' pulled the string fur 'em to take me back. W'en I got into the ship agin I sez to the cap'n, sez I, 'I don't b'lieve we kin do much with that hole.' But he sez to me, sez he, 'W'y, it ain't no crater o' Mount Vesoovus, wot blows things out as fast as ye put 'em in, is't? Now, you jess go down agin an' pass this 'ere line under the ship. We kin haul a big main-sail under an' plug up the hole with that.'

"Waal, I didn' think the skipper's scheme would work, but my business were to do wot he sez. So I tuk the line, an' down I went agin. Wotever indooced me fur to luk around while I were under the ship's bow I don't know, but I did, an' I were not pertiklerly pleased w'en I sees a shark a-risin'. He were a-comin' straight at me from b'low, an' I tell ye I

yanked that string so quick an' hard it were a wonder
I didn't bust it. I were right in front o' the hole at
the time, an' the shark comin' up head on like a gray
streak o' lightnin'. Jess in time the hoistin'-rope
pulled taut, I swung myself away from the hole, an'
as I went up the ship's side wot d' ye think I see?"

"What?" cried the boys.

"The bloomin' shark went head-fust into the
hole, an' there he stuck. He lashed his tale about
an' struggled, but it didn' do no good; 'cos w'y,
them bent-in plates had 'im by the neck, an' he were
caught. I reported this 'ere remarkable condition
o' things to the skipper, an' sez he to we all,

"'By the great horn spoon, boys, our leak are
stopped for us by old Neptune hisself.'

"Howsumever, he sent me down once more to see
ef the shark were still fast, an' ef he quite filled up
the hole. I found that he did, an' I reported so to
Cap'n Waterbury Boggs. So he gives orders right
away to rig the after steam-pumps, an' screw on a
line o' hose to the pipe wot runned through the
bulkhead from the second compartment to the
third. It were a good six hours afore this work
were done, 'cos w'y, everythin' had to be did at
right angles to its proper persition. Howsumever,
it did get finished, an' then it were night an' we had
to stop. We turned out 'arly in the mornin' an'
started up the pumps. The water came through the
hose in great style, an' we got quite jolly a-squirtin'
it out o' the cabin ports.

"Waal, o' course we was all so bloomin' stoopid that we forgot to prepare fur wot were bound to happen. W'en the water got low enough in them two forrard compartments, bang! down came the ship's starn into the water with a smash, an' she war a-ridin' on her keel agin. An' there we was with the steam-pumps screwed up on the side o' one o' the compartments, an' the donkey-engine, too, so that the live coals come a-tumblin' out an' putty near sot the ship afire, not to speak o' us all bein' throwed heels over head w'en the starn dropped. Howsumever, we wasn't badly hurt, an' we got them live coals out putty quick. But we had a sweet job gettin' that donkey-engine down from w'ere it were hung up like a picter on the wall. An' then it took us nigh on to five days to get the cargo to rights agin. Howsumever, we done it, an' then the cap'n headed the ship fur Rio, w'ich were the nearest port, for repairs."

"And what became of the shark?" asked Henry.

"Oh, he stayed right there in the hole till he were pulled out by a powerful tackle in Rio Harbor. An' then he kind o' lay around like dead for a couple o' hours, arter w'ich he shook hisself an' swam around the ship fur a week, till Isaac Hooper, w'ich the same he were fond o' his joke, sez he to me, sez he, 'I b'lieve that there shark are a-waitin' fur to put in his bill for salwage,' sez he to me, jess like that, him bein' fust-mate an' me second."

And the Old Sailor indulged in another of his quaint, silent laughs.

It was one of those beautiful mild mornings of which there are so many in the course of the winter. A moderately brisk wind was blowing off shore, and the Old Sailor was sitting in his favorite place at the end of the pier, gazing out over the ocean. There was not a whitecap in sight, but the vessels which were passing were going at a fine rate of speed. The two boys were standing at the inshore end of the pier for some time before they noticed that the Old Sailor was there. When they saw him they felt sure that he must be looking at some vessel which would remind him of one of his numerous experiences at sea. So they ran down the pier and greeted him with a cheery "Good-morning." As usual, without turning his head, or appearing to be aware of the fact that they were near him, the Old Sailor indulged in one of his quiet laughs, and said, "Waal, and how's the wind this mornin'?"

"I think," said Henry, "that it's pretty nearly due west."

"Werry good," said the Old Sailor, "an' it are just about that, w'ich the same it are a werry good wind for eny wessel wot's goin' down this 'ere coast."

He relapsed into silence, and continued to stare out on the ocean. The boys watched him for a few moments, and finally little George, who could not restrain his impatience, said, "We thought may-be you might see something that would remind you of something."

" W'ich the same I do," said the Old Sailor.

"Then maybe you wouldn't mind telling us what it is?"

" W'ich the same I also would not," answered the Old Sailor. "Mebbe if you wos to look the right way you might see a ship somethin' oncommon."

Both boys looked around the circle of blue water that spread before them, and cried out at once, "I see it!"

The Old Sailor indulged in another of his hearty but silent laughs, and then said, "Wot are it?"

"It is a full-rigged ship," said Henry, "with high top sides, top-gallant poop and forecastle, tumbling-home sides, and a white stripe with false ports painted in. Her flying-jib-boom is sprung, and has a bend in it like our school-teacher's nose. She has old-fashioned single top-sails, and her spanker has three new cloths in it. She is bound south, about four miles off shore, and is doing about seven knots an hour."

The Old Sailor, for the first time, turned his head, and stared at Henry with an expression of admiration.

"Waal, my young friend, you'll be a bloomin' sailor afore your mother; but durin' the course o' my life I seen a good many fellers wot could stan' on a beach an' talk salt, w'ich the same on board ship couldn't tell a marlin'-spike from a slush-bucket. Howsumever, I s'pose it are no more than wot's to be expected after hearin' so many yarns. Waal, that is the werry ship wot I were lookin' at, an' she reminds me o' a woyage wot I took about thirty years ago, w'ich the same time I got into werry high latitoods. Fact is, there ain't no higher latitoods than wot I got to."

"Latitude ends at the north pole, doesn't it?" asked Henry.

"Waal," said the Old Sailor, ignoring the question, "blow me for pickles if this ain't the werry way wot it happened. I were shipped as second-mate on to a wessel called the *Skimmed Milk*, which the same she were the identical picter of that wessel wot you see out yonder. This 'ere *Skimmed Milk* were a sort o' a whaler an' trader mixed. I s'pose they called her *Skimmed Milk* 'cos she were such bloomin' poor quality. Her business were to run up the west coast of Greenland, w'ere she killed whales w'en she saw whales, caught seals w'en there were any, an' traded with the Eskimos for all kinds of truck w'en there were nothin' else to do. I shipped on to her, 'cos havin' been up north oncet I were liable to git the artic fever oncet in a while. Everybody does wot's ever been up there oncet. The

pertiklers of our woyage north ain't no sort of con-
sekence, so I'll just jump over all wot happened till
we got 'way up near the north end of Smith Sound.
We'd got a few whales an' seals, an' done a good
deal of tradin', an' the captain were thinkin' o'
turnin' his head south ; but, bless your heart, one
of the howlin'est gales wot ever blowed just bust
right out o' the south. Pack ice and floes come
tumblin' up with it, an' there wa'n't nothin' for us
to do 'ceptin' to turn tail an' run for the north'ard.
We ran fur two days an' two nights, an' then, while
it were my watch below, smash-bang! the ship
went plum into a iceberg. I were out o' my bunk
an' on deck just in time to tumble into a boat an'
git away from the ship's side, w'en she rolled over
like a dog goin' to sleep an' went down. There wos
six men in that boat besides me, an' we drifted fur
three days. At the end o' that time, not wishing
to make you feel bad, I will say, fur short, that
there were only one man in that boat, an' he were
me. I tried to git to the south, but it war not no
good; so, seein' open water to the north'ard, I let
the boat go that way, hopin' as how I might find
a Eskimo willage somew'ere or other, an' git dogs
an' a sled to take me south to a settlement. I kep'
on goin' north for about five days, an' then the ice
shut in all around me, an' the fust thing I knowed
my boat got nipped an' were smashed into kindlin'
wood. So sez I to myself, sez I, 'There bein' no
water 'ceptin' ice, an' no boat 'ceptin' splinters, I

reckon as how I got to git out an' walk, w'ich the
same it would be better for skatin'.' Now, if I could
'a' seen any shore somew'ere I s'pose I would 'a'
gone ashore, but w'ichever way I looked I couldn't
see nothin' 'cept ice. There were a good deal
more ice nor I wanted; 'cos w'y, such perwisions
as I had would 'a' kep' jess as well without it. So
I started ahead, or prehaps I ought to say afoot,
not knowin' werry well w'ich way I were goin'. It
turned out arterwards that I were goin' north all
the time. I s'pose I needn't tell ye that the weather were putty consid'able cool, so I kep' movin'
putty rapid fur to keep my blood warm. I camped
out on the ice the fust night, an' woke up in the
mornin' so stiff that I almost cracked when I tried
to git up. When I finally did git up, wot do you
s'pose I saw?"

"What?" asked both boys.

"Why, I were afloat on a big ice-floe 'bout a hundred yards square, an' there were water all around
me. 'Waal,' sez I to myself, sez I, 'I was oncet
afloat on a iceberg, but it were bound south, an' I
don't know wot way this 'ere floe is agoin'; howsumever, it don't make no difference wot way it
are goin', 'cos I can't go no other.' 'Long towards
night all kinds of birds lit on my floe, an' some of
'em lit on me. I druv 'em away, 'cos w'y, I kin
stan' a good deal, but I'm blowed if I'll be a chicken-
coop fur snipe. The nex' mornin' w'en I woke up,
an' got the stiffness out o' my joints, I took a look

around. I were still at sea, as you might say, an'
'peared likely to stay there. An' wot do you s'pose
I found sittin' on my floe?"

"I can't imagine," said Henry.

"A bloomin' big seal," said the Old Sailor, "w'ich
the same, w'en I looked at him, he wunk one eye
at me, an' wagged one of his flippers. Then he puts
his head down on the ice, an' begins to cry like a
baby. Nex' he sits up on his tail, hoists his head
up into the air, an' makes a melancholic noise with
his mouth like he thought he were a bloomin' opera-
singer. Sez I to myself, sez I, 'That there seal are
crazy.' Putty soon the seal commenced crawlin'
towards me. I didn't like the way he were actin',
so I backed off. The more I backed off the more
he come on. So sez I to myself, sez I, 'It are got
to be a game of tag between me an' this 'ere fish.'
Sure enough, that's wot it were, 'cos he chased me
around that there floe fur about two hours, till I
got so bloomin' tired I couldn't stand up no more.
So, seein' as how I couldn't stand up, I fell down,
an' then that there measly seal come wobblin' along
the ice an' gave me a boost with his nose an' shoved
me right into the water. Great guns! but it were
cold. O' course I went down, an' w'en I came up
the seal were alongside o' me. Fust thing I knowed
he dived down under me, an' come up so I was sittin' astraddle o' his back. Just as soon as he found
me there he started off across the sea at a ten-knot
gait. O' course there were nothing left for me to

"'SOME OF 'EM LIT ON ME'"

do but to hang on. I couldn't see nothin' at all
'ceptin' white spray, wot flew around me like a
cloud of smoke. Byme-by I got sort o' dizzy, an'
all I could do wos to shut my eyes an' try to stick
on the seal's back, 'cos ef I fell off I'd git drownded.
Well, how long we kep' agoin' I don't know. All
I know is that after a while we fetched up all on a
suddent—that is to say, the seal did. He stopped,
an' I went sailin' up'ards into the air, an' lit on my
back on dry land. I were stunned for a minute,
but I were woke up by a voice sayin' to me, ' Well,
who in thunder are you?'

"I looked up, an' saw a feller sittin' on a rock
smokin' a pipe. He were not putty to look at. He
had a sort o' pale greenish-yaller hair, an' whiskers
o' a similar constitootion wot stuck out all round
his face like the whiskers on a jack-in-the-box. His
nose had been broken, an' one o' his eyes had a droop
to it like a flag w'en there ain't no wind. Soon as
I could git my breath I answered him, an' sez I to
him, sez I,

"'I'm the second-mate o' the ship *Skimmed
Milk.*'

"'Wot!' sez he to me, sez he; 'are there a ship
up here?'

"'No,' sez I to him, sez I; 'she are down there,'
w'ich the same I pointed to the bottom of the sea.

"'Oh!' sez he to me, 'I feel better. I don't want
nobody comin' up here to steal my pole.'

"'Wot pole?' sez I.

"'The one up yonder,' sez he.

"I looked w'ere he pointed, an' saw a tall flag-staff with the English flag flying on it. I didn't see no reason w'y any one should want to steal that pole. But not wishin' to be disagreeable, I sez to him:

"'There ain't nobody comin' but me, an' I would-n't 'a' come if I could 'a' helped it; but that there bloomin' seal, after doin' some circus tricks, shoved me into the water, dropped me on his back, an' brung me here whether I wanted to be brung or not. That are the most pertricklerest seal I ever saw.'

"'Oh,' sez he, laughin', 'that are my trained seal.'

"'Did you train him yourself?'

"'No,' sez he. 'He were a trained seal in a American circus. He were bein' took to London with the show, an' he were kep' in a tank on deck. One day in a gale a big sea come aboard the ship an' washed him overboard. The minute he struck the ocean he made a bee-line for his own home up near Lady Franklin Bay.'

"'W'ere did you git him?'

"'I ran acrost him in that bay on my way up here, an' I knowed him by his tricks, 'cos I'd seen him in the show in New York. He are a werry useful animal, are that seal, an' anythin' wot he finds adrift he brings right in to me.'

"'You 'ain't told me who you wos yet.'

"'Oh,' sez the man, 'I'm just a plain every-day sailor-man like yourself.'

" 'How did you git here?'

" 'That's wot I don't tell,' sez he, lookin' werry cunnin'.

" 'An' do you live here?'

" 'Yes,' sez he to me, sez he, 'I live here all the year round, right on this little island; an' mind you, it ain't near so bad as you might think. It are not near so cold as it are five hundred miles further south, an' the fishin' an' shootin' is bully.'

" 'Still,' sez I to him, sez I, 'I don't see w'y you stay here.'

" 'Oh,' sez he to me, sez he, 'I don't dare go away.'

" 'W'y not?' sez I.

" ''Cos,' sez he, 'if I did, somebody would come an' steal my pole.'

" 'W'y,' sez I to him, sez I, 'I don't see nothin' wonderful about that there pole. Wot for should anybody want to steal it?'

" 'W'y, blow me!' sez he; 'that are the north pole.'

" 'Waal,' sez I to him, sez I, 'you don't expect an old sailor like me to b'lieve that the pole are really a stick stickin' up out o' the end o' the earth, do you?'

" 'Oh no,' sez he to me, sez he, laughin'; 'that stick ain't the pole. That's a stick I stuck into the spot w'ere the pole is so as to h'ist the English flag over it, an' claim the discovery in her majesty's name.'

" 'Waal, now that you've discovered it,' sez I, 'w'y don't you go home an' tell about it?'

" 'How kin I?' sez he.   'Soon as I go away some other feller like you will come up here and steal the north pole from me.'

" 'W'y,' sez I to him, sez I, 'if you wos gone an' I were here alone, I wouldn't be a bit better off than you wos afore I come.'

" 'That's all right,' sez he; 'but how were I to know that a whole boatload of men wouldn't come here some day an' find this pole?'

" 'Then wot are you goin' to do?'

" 'I'm goin' to stay right here, hold on to this pole, an' keep the English flag a-flyin' over it till somebody comes an' finds me here.'

" 'Waal,' sez I, 'it seems to me that somebody has come an' found you here.'

" 'An' will you play square an' go back an' tell folks that John B. Smith, of Yarmouth, has discovered the north pole, an' is a-holdin' on to it for all he's worth?'

" 'You kin bet your entire possessions,' sez I to him, sez I, 'that if ever I get back to a place where there's less latitood an' more longitood than there is up here, w'ere there is all the latitood you kin git an' 'ain't no longitood at all, I'll send somebody up to find you.'

" 'Waal,' sez he, 'there won't be no trouble about your gittin' back.'

" With that he whistles two or three times, an' the seal come swimmin' up, an' wunk his eye an' shook his flipper at him.

"'Go git the boat,' sez he to the seal, sez he.

"The seal swum away, an' then I sez to John B. Smith, sez I,

"'Perhaps you wouldn't mind givin' me some dry clothes.'

"Waal, to make the story short, he fixed me out with dry clothes, an' then the seal come swimmin' round, towin' a good‑sized yawl‑boat. John B. Smith an' me loaded her with perwisions, an' then I got aboard. I shook hands with Smith, an' sez I to him, sez I, 'Good-bye; an' I hope no one will steal your pole while you are asleep.'

"'Good-bye,' sez he. 'Be sure you send up a relief party.'

"I jumped into the boat, an' off the seal went, towin' me to the south at a twelve-knot gait. He never let up on towin' me till we come in sight o' a whaler in Smith Sound. Then the bloomin' seal wouldn't go no further, an' he wouldn't let me take the boat. So I got out an' walked across the ice, an' waved my coat till the ship saw me an' sent a boat for me, an' that's the way I got back from the north pole."

"And did you send a relief party?" asked Henry.

"Waal, I been tellin' this story ever since I got back; but do you know wot?"

"Well, what?" said Henry.

"I can't git nobody to b'lieve me."

And shaking his head mournfully the Old Sailor walked slowly away.

HOW I BECAME AN ADMIRAL

It was a clear and bracing November morning. The off-shore wind was light but steady, so that the big three-masted schooners climbing upward towards Sandy Hook had aloft their staysails, and were gliding nobly along at a six-knot gait. Here and there in the middle distance dancing black spots on the steel-gray sea showed where the hardy cod-fisherman was at his chilling toil. Ever and anon a dull whir called the eye to masses of mottled coots cleaving their way southward. But it was not upon any of these familiar sights that the steady glance of the Old Sailor was fixed as he balanced himself on his sturdy legs near the end of the pier. He was gazing with the deepest interest upon a steamer which was churning the water into tangled swirls of silver and emerald-green under her stern, and tossing it in fountains of sunlit white under her forefoot as she clove her way towards lower latitudes.

"He looks excited," said Henry.

"Let's go and find out what's the matter," said George. And the two boys ran down the pier with a merry clatter of nimble feet.

"An' how's the wind to-day?" asked the Old Sailor, without turning his head.

"West by north," answered Henry.

"Werry good, too. An' wot's that out yonder?"

"Why, a steamer, of course," said George.

"Of course, sez you. An' wot kind o' a steamer?"

"I don't know," said Henry; "I can't quite make out her flag. It looks like a green one with a yellow diamond in it."

"Werry good; werry good. You'll be able to see round a corner yet. An' wot's that on her fo'c's'le deck?"

"Why, it looks like a big cannon!" exclaimed George.

"So it are, my son; an' the flag are the flag o' Brayzil; an' the wessel are the new cruiser *Nigtheroy*, an' she are boun' 'way down fur Rio to smash Admiral Mello."

The boys now were deeply interested.

"Ah me!" exclaimed the Old Sailor; "she are ossifered by Americans, an' that reminds me o' the time a Kimee ship had a American admiral, w'ich the same I were him."

"Oh, do tell us about that!" exclaimed Henry.

"That are the werry identical thing wot I'm a-goin' fur to do," said the Old Sailor.

"Waal," he continued, after a momentary pause, "you may call me a landsman ef this 'ere aren't the way wot it come about. I were fust-mate o' the brig

10

Sky Blue Jones, boun' from Lewes fur Durban with
a cargo o' Noo Jarsec moskeeters—"

"Oh, please wait!" said George. "What did they
want of mosquitoes at Durban?"

"W'y, the natyves uses 'em to cure bilious fevers,
w'ich the same their bites is werry good fur. Bilious fevers rages on them coasts owin' to the natyves a-livin' mostly on ostridges' eggs poached in
goats' milk, an' that are werry bilious purwision, as
them knows wot has tried it. Howsumever, that
ain't got nothin' to do with this 'ere yarn wot I'm
a-tellin' ye. The *Sky Blue Jones* had werry good
weather till she got 'way down b'low the line, an'
then it come on to blow consid'able from the no'theast. Fur the fust two days it wa'n't no more'n
a ordinary gale, an' we was able fur to run to the
south'ard, a-keepin' o' the wind an' sea on our port
quarter. But the cap'n he sez to me, sez he, 'The
glass are a-fallin' all the time, so look out fur
squalls.' On the third day it blowed a giniwine
hurricane, an' we hove the brig to on the port tack.
The leeway an' drift was somethin' dreadful, an' by
the follerin' noon we didn't have no putty good idee
w'ere we was. It blowed all that day an' all that
night, an' jess after daybreak the next day one o'
the hands yelled, 'Land ho!' Sure 'nuff, there it
were, right under our lee, with half a mile o' surf
outside to show that there wos shoals an' reefs.
'We're a goner,' sez the cap'n to me, sez he; 'them's
the Kimee Islan's, an' ef we ain't drownded we'll be

made slaves.' W'ich the same it was not werry encouragin' fur to hear."

" Where are the Kimee Islands?" asked Henry.

" Latitood 29° south an' longitood 37° west. Leastways that's as near as I ever knowed w'ere they was ; but I never could find 'em on the chart. Waal, to make this 'ere yarn shorter, I mought as well say that the *Sky Blue Jones* struck the outer reefs bow on, an' the next minute a tremenjous sea swep' over her, an' I were carried overboard. I don't reckomember werry much o' the subsekent perceedin's till I found myself a-layin' on to the beach an' a delegation o' savidges a-dancin' a hornpipe around me. As soon as they seed I were come to, they poured some kind o' a peppery drink down my throat, an' I felt better right away. Then they set me on my feet an' started me inland. I wanted to know wot 'd become o' my shipmates, an' the savidges made me onderstan' by signs that they wos all drownded. You may be sure I didn't feel werry happy, an' I wanted to sit right down. But a werry tall savidge, with a lady's fur boa tied around his waist an' a old leather hat-box on to his head, prodded me with his spear, an' sez he to me, sez he, ' No sit ; walk.' So I jess walked. I found arterward that this 'ere savidge could speak English putty well, as he'd been on exhibition once in a museum in England. They marched me off to their willage, w'ich the same it were nothin' but a lot o' tents made out o' hides. The nex' day they put me to work a-poundin' dried cocoanut up fur flour. It were the only kind o' flour they knowed anythin' about. I might 'a' been there yet ef it hadn't been fur the war wot I got to be a admiral in.

"Ye see," continued the Old Sailor, after another glance at the *Nictheroy,* now well to the southward, "the Kimee Islands was divided into two parts, an' the chiefs o' the two parts was mortal inimies, owin' to one o' them havin' stole from t'other the only plug-hat wot ever come ashore from a wrack there. He stole the box too, an' wore that fur his every-day hat. The other chief were allus a-tryin' to git that hat back, an' so Pusowynee, the feller wot had it —an' also me—were allus in hot water. Arter I'd bin there about two months an' had braced up Pusowynee's English so that him an' me could conwarse putty good, old Thakelbolen, the other chief, made one o' his attacks. Waal, it were more fun than a dog-fight. Old Thakelbolen, wearin' a woman's blue sailor-hat wi' a red feather in't, a gridiron for a breastplate, an' a umbrella cover wi' the ribs into 't yet fur a skirt, comes over in a big war canoe, paddled by a dozen savidges. He were followed by a dozen other canoes all loaded with Kimees. An' how do you s'pose them fellers fout?"

"Why, how?" asked both boys.

"They throwed things at one another! Honest! They throwed spears an' stones, w'ich the same them canoes was loaded with. An' they could throw mighty hard an' straight, too. O' course they didn't

kill werry many on neither side, but they wounded
a lot. Pusowynee, ye see, got out his canoes an'
went to meet 'em, an' this 'ere remarkable naval
battle took place outside o' the reefs in the open
water. Waal, arter two hours o' hard fightin' Thakelbolen an' his gang had to sheer off, 'cos they didn't
have nothin' more to throw, an' Pusowynee he
wouldn't run away. W'en the chief come ashore
he had lumps all over him w'ere he'd bin hit, an' a
hole in the leather hat-box, w'ere Thakelbolen hisself had sent a spear through 't. He were putty
mad, were Pusowynee, an' sez he to me, sez he,
'Nex' time I go I kill him, sure.' Pusowynee were
a werry pertikler man sometimes.

"Howsumever, that night w'en I were in my
bunk, w'ich the same were a soft spot on the ground,
I thort the thing over, an' sez I to myself, sez I, 'I
reckon I kin l'arn Pusowynee a thing or two, an'
prehaps he'll be so grateful he'll let me go.' Ye see,
them there savidges never used sails on to their canoes 'ceptin' w'en they wos runnin' dead afore the
wind; 'cos w'y, their canoes made so much leeway
w'en they tried to sail 'em any other way. So I sez
to Pusowynee, sez I, 'W'y don't ye put a centre-
board into your canoe so's ye can sail to windward?'
Waal, he looked at me a minute an' then shook
his head. 'You gone crazy, eh?' he sez to me, sez
he. 'Not much,' sez I to he, sez I; 'you gimme a
canoe an' let me fix her up an' I'll show you.'
Waal, he didn' seem to think there'd be no harm

in a-givin' me a canoe to play with, an' so he gave
me one about twenty-five foot long. In about two
days I had a centre - board into her, an' I inwited
the chief to take a sail. The wind were a-blowin'
dead on shore, an' about three-quarters o' a mile to
wind'ard were a big rock stickin' out o' the sea.
Sez I to he, sez I, 'Can I sail to that rock?' Sez he
to me, sez he, 'No; wind blow us back.' Then sez
I to he, sez I, 'Watch us get there,' jess like that,
him bein' a chief an' me a miseracious pris'ner. I
got under way on the port tack, an' as soon as I
headed the canoe up within about five points o' the
wind, Pusowynee nearly had a fit. 'Canoe go backward!' he shouted. 'Not much!' sez I. An' w'en
I went about an' headed her dead fur the rock on
the starb'rd tack, he blame nigh jumped overboard.
On the run back I explained the principle o' the
centre-board to him. W'en we jumped ashore, all
the savidges set up a yell and waved their spears,
an' Pusowynee then an' there app'inted me chief o'
his war canoes, w'ich were the same as bein' admiral
o' the fleet. I spent a couple o' weeks in fittin' 'em
all out with centre-boards. Then news come that
old Thakelbolen were approachin' with a fair wind.
We got our fleet under way. I had already showed
a lot o' the savidges how to sail to wind'ard, an' we
beat up to meet Thakelbolen. Waal, w'en he seed
us zigzaggin' up ag'in' the wind, he were clean flabbergasted, an' his warriors begin to yell, 'Hovelko!
hovelko!' W'ich the same in the Kimee langwidge

means 'Magic.' Old Pusowynee he jess laid down
in the bottom o' the canoe an' had a fit a-laughin'.
'Thakelbolen heap scared!' he screeched. But the
nex' thing we knowed old Thak an' his fleet jess
turned tail an' begin to paddle straight back. Now
ye can paddle a canoe dead to wind'ard, but ye can't
sail that way. So Thakelbolen putty soon begin to
get away from us. Waal, that settled the whole
business with Pusowynee.

"'Centel-board no good!' he yelled. 'White slave
bad man! Take down him sail! Paddle! Paddle
hard!'

"But it wasn't any good. Thakelbolen had a
good lead, an', besides, all the centre-boards was
a-draggin' under our canoes an' a-holdin' 'em back.
Pusowynee he looked as if he would eat me, an' I
made up my mind that I were as good as cooked.
Howsumever, I got off with fifty lashes; but Pusowynee had all the centre-boards took out o' the canoes as soon as he got ashore. It were werry lucky
fur me that the canoe he lent me were a-lyin' all by
herself in a little cove about a mile up the beach, an'
so her centre-board stayed in; 'cos w'y, she were furgot. Waal, Pusowynee he jess piled the work on to
me arter that, an' I got putty much down in the
mouth, till all on a suddent one night a idea come to
me. Every mornin' arter that I turned out extra 'arly,
an' managed to do a little work on my own hook
down in the woods near the beach. I'd made up my
mind to show Pusowynee a way to throw bigger

stones, an' throw 'em furder 'n old Thak could.   I
reckoned to rig up a scheme to sink his canoes."

"How?" inquired both boys.

"That are the werry identical thing wot I'm
a-goin' fur to tell ye.   Oncet upon a time I heerd o'
monkeys bendin' down cocoanut-trees an' lettin' 'em
fly up agin so they chucked the nuts half a mile.
So I picked out a nice stout young tree, an' trimmed
off all the branches.   Then I built a sort o' a box
up near the top o' the tree, facin' to the sea.   Arter
that I hunted up some rope an' blocks wot 'd come
ashore from the brig.   I put a lashin' 'round the tree
jess b'low the box, an' hooked a block into 't.   Then
I rove my rope through the block, an' agin through
a snatch-block made fast to the foot o' another
tree.   I hauled down the top o' the tree, the young
trunk bendin' like a fine bow.   Now I seed that ef I
let 'er go I'd soon bust my block all to pieces with
the slashin' around it 'd git.   So I rigged a kind o'
trigger, like ye put on a rabbit snare, to hold the
tree down.   I put a stone weighin' about thirty
pound inter the box, onhooked my block an' fall, an'
pulled the trigger.   Waal, that stone whistled like
a cannon-ball w'en it went off.   It whizzed out to
sea a good 500 yards, an' then skipped three or four
times, an' sank.   The nex' day I begged fur a audi-
ence with Pusowynee, but he sent word back that
he didn' want no more centre-boards.   Lucky fur
me, I'd made friends with one o' his right-hand men,
an' I got him to go an' see my stone-chucker."

" ' AWAY WENT THE STONE—AN' ALSO PUSOWYNEE ' "

"The ancients called them catapults," said Henry.

"Well, mebbe," answered the Old Sailor; "but I guess nobody but a sailor-man would 'a' thort o' this scheme. Nex' day the chief came to see 't, an' he danced a war-dance. 'Now kill Thakelbolen from shore! No go in centre-board canoe! Good!' he sez. Then I told him I could make bigger ones than this, ef he would gimme crews to handle 'em. He agreed, an' in a few days I had five o' them— wot d' ye call 'em?—catterpulps all ready fur old Thakelbolen. The werry nex' day old Thak's fleet o' canoes was seen a-comin'. Pusowynee allowed that this were a-goin' to be the greatest day o' his life. So he got out the sacred plug-hat. Thakel- bolen didn' know wot to make o' our not comin' out to meet him, an' he brought his fleet to 'bout four hundred yards off, an' set up a loud yellin'. Pusowynee tips me the nod, an' I lets go a hundred- pound stone, w'ich the same hits one o' Thak's canoes an' smashes in one side. The water ran in an' the ca- noe turned over, dumpin' the savidges into the sea. Thak an' his forces was jess stunned by this new freak, an' they couldn't move. 'Now kill! Now kill!' yelled Pusowynee. So we lets go the whole broadside, an' w'en the spray cleared away there were only one canoe left, an' that were the flag- ship, with Thakelbolen in command. 'Kill quick!' screamed Pusowynee. We hauled down our big- gest tree, an' hoisted in a 300-pounder. Pusowy- nee got so excited that he jumped forrard to onhook the block an' fall hisself. At that blessed minnit the feller at the trigger got out o' his senses, an' pulled without orders. Swish! Up went the tree, away went the stone—an' also Pusowynee!

"We seed him a-sailin' thro' the air, holdin' the sacred plug-hat on with both hands, an' a-turnin' more somersets than a Fourth-o'-July pinwheel. The stone fell short, but Pusowynee went ca-plump into the middle o' Thakelbolen's canoe, w'ere he laid senseless, w'ile old Thak grabbed the sacred plug-hat, put it on his own head with a yell of victory, an' then went off at full speed fur home, with Pusowynee a prisoner."

The Old Sailor paused for a minute, after which he resumed, with the deepest solemnity:

"Boys, I took adwantage o' the subsekent confusion to git into the woods as fast as my legs would carry me. I loaded my canoe with cocoanuts, an' that night, as soon as it were dark, I got under way with a brisk westerly wind, an' stood to the no'theast. I were picked up two days later by the English cruiser *Australia*, an' landed at Gibraltar, w'ere I shipped fur London on a collier. An' so I got back to Ameriky."

It was a clear, cool summer morning, and the Old Sailor sat in his customary place at the end of the pier. The two boys were sitting beside him. All three were gazing out on the ocean. The long glassy swells rolled lazily in, and shattered themselves into fragments of flashing silver against the hard yellow beach. A stately fish-hawk soared high above, a floating silhouette against the clear blue sky. Far out to the eastward a magnificent full-rigged ship with double top-sails and top-gallants rolled slowly as she vainly strove to make her way to the southward in the light air. Nearer to the land two steamers were tearing the water into clouds of smokelike spray as they hurried down the coast. Heavy columns of black smoke showed that the stokers hidden away in the dark recesses below were spreading fresh coal on the fires.

"S'posin' I wos to ax you," said the Old Sailor, suddenly, "wot them there two steamers wos a-doin', wot 'd you say?"

"I'd say that they were firing up," answered Henry, confidently.

"Werry good," said the Old Sailor — "werry

good as fur as it goes. But wot are they a-firin' up fur ?"

" Because they're in a hurry," said little George.

" Also, moreover, an' likewise werry good too. But howsumever ye 'ain't hit the p'int yit."

" Won't you tell us what the point is?" said Henry.

" That are the werry identical thing wot I'm about to go fur to come fur to do," answered the Old Sailor. " Ye see them there two steamers is a-startin' on a race."

" Oh !" exclaimed both boys.

" Edzackly—oh," continued the Old Sailor, gravely. Then, after a moment of silence, he unexpectedly continued : " W'ich the same it reminds me o' the v'yage I made on the tramp-steamer *Pickled Pepper* from Constantinople to Noo Yawk in the year 1878."

" Please tell us about it," said the boys.

" ' Ain't you two boys knowed me long enough to know that w'en I gits reminded o' suthin' I allus tells ye about it ? Wot else 's the use o' gittin' reminded ? Anyhow, s' help me Sally Growler, ef this ain't the way wot it happened. The *Pickled Pepper* had taken on a cargo o' ottomans. Do ye know wot a ottoman are ?"

" It's a sofa without a back, isn't it ?"

" Werry good. It aren't got no back an' consequentially no backbone, w'ich are w'y it's like Turkey, an' that are w'y it are called the Ottoman Empire. Ottomans was all the rage in 1878, an' the genooine ones from Turkey was a-sellin' like hot cakes. The steamer *P. W. Murphy* were a-loadin' with 'em at the same time we was, an' we knowed there were a-goin' to be a scrimmage to see who'd git to Noo Yawk fust. 'Cos w'y, ef we both got in at onect an' dumped all our ottomans on to the market, the price 'd go down. But ef we could git in a day or two ahead, the firm wot were a-goin' to take our ottomans could git 'em all sold off afore the *P. W. Murphy* could discharge her cargo. Well, as luck 'd have it, jess as we wos a-gittin' the last o' our cargo aboard, somethin' busted down in the engine-room. The engineer said as how it would take twenty-four hours to repair it, so the *P. W. Murphy* got to sea six hours ahead o' us. That made our cap'n b'ilin' mad. As soon as we started he shouts down the tube to the engineer, 'Shove the old kettle through it till her sides smoke ; we got to beat that Irish tramp to Sandy Hook.' An' the engineer he sez to the cap'n, sez he, ' Werry good, sir ; it should be did.'

"Putty soon a most outrageous black smoke come a-rollin' up out o' the funnels. 'That's business,' sez the cap'n ; 'but goodness gracious, wot a lot o' soot are a-fallin'!' Sure 'nuff, the soot beginned fur to come down out o' that smoke like it were black snow, an' putty soon the whole deck abaft the smoke-stack were covered with it two inches deep. The cap'n he calls the bo'sun's mate, an'

tells him to git a gang o' men an' shovel it off, an'
then he calls down to the engineer, an' sez he to
him, sez he, ' Wot on 'arth are you a-burnin' ?'   An'
the engineer sez he to him, sez he : 'It's that bloomin' Turkish coal.   I think they've swindled us.   We
bought it at the same place as the *P. W. Murphy,* though.'   Then the cap'n danced an' used hard
words.   'Them fellows has paid the coal - man to
sell us bad coal, but we'll beat 'em anyhow.'   So he
ordered the engineer to pile on the coal, an' not
stop to worry about w'ether it 'd last till we got to
port, an' he told him to tie down the safety-valve.
' We'll bust our b'ilers an' all go to Davy Jones's
locker afore we git beat,' sez the cap'n.   ' Werry
good, sir,' sez the engineer to him, sez he ; 'Davy
Jones's locker are our port, ef yer sez so.'   An'
then the smoke beginned fur to git wuss an' wuss.
We was all busy tryin' to sweep the soot off the
deck, but we could hear the awful rumpus the engines was a-makin' down below.   I made up my
mind that Davy Jones's locker were close aboard o'
us, but it turned out that we wosn't bound there,
arter all.

"It were daylight the fourth day w'en the *P. W.
Murphy* were sighted dead ahead o' us.   She were
about ten miles away, an' so we'd gained a good
fifty mile on her.   'Cos w'y, we reckoned that her
best speed were about ten knots, an' we'd got up to
a p'int ten miles astern arter her leavin' six hours
ahead o' us.   Well, mebbe that 'ere *P. W. Murphy*

weren't a-hustlin'. She sart'nly were. W'y, the
water were a-flyin' a dozen feet high under her
starn w'ere the perpeller were a-slashin' it. But,
ye see, the wessel's lines wos so full that she couldn't
be druv no faster. An' now it come to a question
o' who could keep up the strain best an' longest.

"'Put suthin' greasy on to your fires,' calls our
cap'n down to the engineer.

"'All right, sir,' sez the engineer, sez he. 'We
got two hundred Cincinnati hams in our stores.
How'll them do?'

"'Let the cook cut all the fat off 'em, an' heave
it in.'

"'Werry good,' sez the engineer, sez he. An' in
half an hour light blue smoke beginned fur to come
up out o' the smoke stack, an' dear, dear, wot a dreadful smell! Next thing we knowed the same kind o'
smoke were a-comin' from the *P. W. Murphy.*

"'They're a-burnin' their hams, too,' sez the cap'n,
'but we'll beat 'em at that game.'

"Then he ordered the ship's carpenter to broach
the paint-room stores, an' in a few minutes the stokers was a-firin' up with raw an' boiled linseed-oil,
turpentine, Japan, mineral paint, an' patent drier.
My eye, you never see nothin' burn like that patent
drier! It made the fire so hot that the engineer
called up through the tube.

"'The steam's too much heated; it's makin' the
cylinders red-hot!'

"'Turn the hose on 'em,' sez the cap'n, sez he.

'We got to beat that bloomin' tramp, an' there mustn't be no accidents.'

"The perpeller were a-thrashin' away mos' dreadful, w'en all on a suddent there were a jolt, an' the engineer reports that one blade were bruk off the screw.

"'Make her go around faster, then,' sez the cap'n.

"'Then I got to have more fire,' sez the engineer.

"'Send down the top-gallant-yards,' sez the cap'n, 'an' w'en them's gone give him the tops'l-yards. I'll burn all the wood on the consarned ole hooker, but I will catch the *P. W. Murphy*.'

"The yards wos lowered an' chopped up, an' byme-by we got orders to give the stokers the topmasts. The lower-masts was iron, so they couldn't burn them; but we unrove all the riggin' wot were made o' tarred rope, an' that went into the fire too. The furnaces wos red-hot now, an' hands wos a-standin' by heavin' water on 'em to keep 'em from meltin.' Every half-hour the steward went 'round an' put ice on the heads o' the engineers an' stokers, or else they'd 'a' died right at their posts. The thermometer were 170° in the fire-room. Fust thing we knowed there were another jolt, an' the engineer calls up,

"'Another blade are gone, sir.'

"'Turn the bloomin' thing around faster,' sez the cap'n, sez he.

"'Gimme more fire!' yells the engineer.

" ' Rip out the cabin bulkheads,' sez the cap'n.

" Bang ! went the axes, an' we commenced choppin' the ship apart.

" ' I wonder ef we're a-gainin' any on to her,' sez the cap'n.

" Then he sends for his sextant, an' he takes the altitood o' the *P. W. Murphy's* water - line, an' he sez, sez he :

" ' We ain't a-gainin' a bloomin' foot on to her. We got to make more steam an' drive that one blade faster or bust our b'ilers in the attempt.'

" ' Werry good, sir,' sez the mate, w'ich he were me. ' Wot shall we burn next?'

" ' The deck-houses an' the boats. Let 'er go !'

" An' accordin' to orders I lets 'er go, fur I seed now that the cap'n was bound to win, ef he had to jump into the furnace hisself. This 'ere race wot I'm a-tellin' you 'bout had now been goin' on several days, an' we was more'n half-way across. The *P. W. Murphy* were still about ten mile ahead o' us. All at oncet she stopped.

" ' Quick ! Quick !' yells the cap'n ; ' git me my glass, till I see wot's the matter with her.'

" I fetched him the glass, an' he took a squint. Then he ups an' slams the glass down on the deck, an' knocked it so crooked you could see round turns in the horizon line.

" ' They've come across a dirilict loaded with wood, an' they're a-gittin' of 't aboard !' sez he to me, sez he.

11

"'Werry good, sir; but all the time we're a-runnin' up on to her hand over hand,' sez I to he, sez I, jess like that, him bein' cap'n an' me mate.

"'But you howlin' old idiot,' sez he to me, sez he, 'we're a-burnin' up the ship under our werry feet!'

"'We ain't a-burnin' the engine an' the screw,' sez I to he, sez I.

"'You're a loonatic,' sez he, dancin' round like his feet hurt him.

"'It are so hot down here that the men can't stand,' comes up from the engine-room.

"'Turn a hose on 'em an' cool 'em off,' sez the cap'n.

"'But that'll fill the engine-room with water.'

"'Bail it out, then!'

"I made up my mind the cap'n were gone crazy, an' I'd have to stand by to save the ship. The *P. W. Murphy* knocked off takin' on wood w'en we got about two mile astern o' her, an' beginned ploughing ahead agin at a ten-knot gait. She hadn't burnt up her yards nor nothin', but she'd sent all her spars down, so as to be on even tarmes with us.

"'Can't ye drive that thing around faster?' yells the cap'n down to the engine-room agin.

"'No, our fire's gittin' low.'

"'Rip up the deck!' sez the cap'n.

"'All hands rip up deck!' yells the bo'sun's mate.

"The men stared a bit, an' then fell to with axes an' hatchets, an' the plankin' beginned fur to come up. It were good fat Georgy pine, an', my lands,

"CAN'T, EH? CAN'T?"

how 't did burn! We piled that on, an' then the steward came on deck, an' sez he to the cap'n, sez he,

" ' We got lots o' sugar an' molasses an' sweet-oil an' putty consid'able kerosene in the stores.'

" ' W'y on 'arth didn't ye tell us that afore ?' screamed the cap'n. ' Put 'em all in the furnace fires.'

" Ten minutes arterwards he hollers down to the engineer :

" ' How are your fires now ? Hot 'nuff ?'

" ' Too hot! The iron plates in the ship's sides is a-meltin'.'

" ' Let 'em melt an' be blowed!' sez the cap'n.

" ' But this 'ere wessel 'll sink,' sez I to he, sez I.

" ' Who 'n Jerusalem cares ?' sez he to me, jess like that.

" ' But we can't get the cargo to port ef the ship sinks,' sez I to he.

" ' Can't, eh—can't ? Call yourself an old sailor ? You watch me, an' I'll show ye how we can get this 'ere cargo into port.'

" Then he orders the bo'sun's mate to take all hands b'low an' pack them ottomans down into the lower hold.

" ' Cut away all the bulkheads,' sez he, ' an' run the ottomans in solid from stem to starn. Then git all the wire riggin' aboard an' lash 'em together, so they can't possibly come apart.'

" The hands jumped b'low to do w'at he'd told 'em.

All this time the ship were a-reelin' an' a-tremblin'
like she had a fit. But we was a-gainin' on the *P.
W. Murphy.* Half an hour later we passed her.
All hands was called on deck to cheer. But the engineer he yells up the tube,

"'All the bolts in the wessel's frames is melted
out, an' I spect she'll fall apart.'

"'Let 'er go!' yells the cap'n. 'All hands b'low!'

"He jumped off the bridge an' tumbled down
into the hold. We all follered, even the man at the
wheel. The next minute there were a crash an' a
tremenjous sizzlin', an' the old ship jess opened out
like a piece o' paper wot's bin folded. There were
nothin' left to hold her together, an' her iron sides
flattened out an' went steamin' an' bubblin' down
into the sea. An' then we all seed the cap'n's idee.
Fur we found ourselves afloat on them there ottomans, an', bless your souls, so were the furnaces an'
the engines an' the shaft an' the perpeller! All the
time we'd been so excited that we didn't know
w'ere we wos, but now we seed that we wos not
more'n twenty miles off Sandy Hook. At that
werry minute blow me fur pickles ef there weren't
a tremenjous explogion, an' we seed that the *P. W.
Murphy* had bust her b'ilers!

"'Hooray!' sez the cap'n.

"'Hooray!' sez us.

"At that there were a jolt an' a wobble, an' wot
d'ye think?"

"What?" asked the boys, breathlessly.

" The rest o' our perpeller were gone.

" ' Stick a ottoman on to the shaft!' sez the cap'n.

" No sooner said than done, an' the whole crew putty nigh died a-laffin' to see that Turkish sofa thrashin' the water. But it kep' us goin' ahead, an' byme-by we got a tug an' was towed up the harbor, an' got our cargo landed twelve hours ahead o' the *P. W. Murphy.*"

" A great victory!" exclaimed Henry.

" Not so werry, either," said the Old Sailor, solemnly. " 'Cos w'y, they went an' discharged me an' the cap'n fur gittin' the goods damidged by water!"

THE UNSINKABLE PILOT-BOAT

It was a warm hazy day in August. The air seemed to be saturated with moisture, and yet full of heat. Looking out to sea one could trace the progress of successive showers by straight columns of deep neutral tint which seemed to move around the horizon with solemn dignity. Here and there patches of grayish mist obscured the rim of the sea, and gave a surprising appearance of steam rising from the water. The ocean itself was a dozen different colors by reason of the many varieties of sky reflected in its waters. There was almost no wind at all, and the swells ran in oily, silent, snakelike undulations to the beach, where they broke with an angry serpentine hissing. Vessels came and went from the curtains of shifting mist like ghosts walking upon the water. Altogether it was an uncanny morning, yet one full of interest to the lover of marine views. The Old Sailor was sitting, as usual, at the end of the pier, gazing out to sea, as if his vision by mere force of steadiness could penetrate fog or rain and discover what lay beyond. The two boys, clad in rubber boots and coats, came down the pier quietly, for they were more than half afraid that their friend might at any moment rise and depart, owing to the wetness of the weather. But the Old Sailor sat and smoked, and paid no attention to the elements. The boys went and sat down beside him, and he acted as if he were unaware of their presence; but they were so well acquainted with his peculiarities that they simply sat still and waited. Presently a schooner emerged from a fog-bank, and, rolling quickly on the swells, stood in towards the shore.

"An' wot kind o' a wessel mought that be?" asked the Old Sailor, without turning his head.

"A pilot-boat," answered both boys, promptly.

"An' how d' ye know she are a pilot-boat?"

"By the number painted on her main-sail," answered Henry.

"Werry good, too. W'ich the same she are a-headin' fur the beach like as ef she wos a-goin' fur to run ashore."

"But she won't, will she?" asked George.

"I reckon not," said the Old Sailor; "but I don't preesume that it would do her so werry much damidge ef she did."

"Why not?" inquired Henry.

"Cos w'y," replied the Old Sailor, "you can't do much damidge to them 'ere boats. There ain't no safer craft a-floatin' on to the surface o' that 'ere mill-pond out yender. W'y, ye can't sink 'em."

"Can't sink them?" repeated Henry.

"In course not. I seen it tried."

"When?"

"Waal, ye may tie my feet 'round my neck an' make a human grommet out o' me ef this 'ere ain't the werry identical way wot it happened : I were a-knockin' aroun' Noo Yawk one fall without no berth, an' I beginned fur to get putty hungry. So sez I to myself, sez I, I guess I'd better ship on the fust thing as comes along. I were a-walkin' along the East River at the time an' I seed a pilot-boat a-layin' alongside o' a pier. To make this 'ere yarn wot I'm a-tellin' you short, I shipped aboard her as a foremast hand. Her name were the *Sam an' Sally*, No. 22½. Waal, nothin' werry pertikler happened ontil winter weather come on, an' then we had the time wot I'm a-goin' fur to tell you about. The weather come on so cold that the spray used to freeze in the air as it come over the bows an' fall on to the deck in small chunks o' ice like hailstuns. Then it begins fur to blow putty fresh, an' our hull begins to ice up. It weren't more'n twenty-four hours afore we had a casin' o' ice all 'round us about two inches thick. Meanwhile the riggin' were gittin' wet an' freezin' harder'n iron, so that w'en the order come fur to put the second reef into the main-s'l, w'y, ye couldn't do anything at all with the bloomin' thing. The halyards wouldn't render thro' the blocks, 'cos w'y, they wos frozen like ramrods. An' the reef-p'ints wos as solid as kitchen pokers, an' jess about as easy fur to bend. So ole Pete Murphy, the boss pilot, he sez, sez he, 'Let her go, an' see wot she'll do.' Waal, she heeled over

like one o' them slantin'-backed rockin'-cheers wot
your ma has, an' she shoved her nose into it mos'
ridiklous. I sez to Pete Murphy, sez I, 'Cap, this
'ere schooner are a-gittin' werry much down by the
head on account o' the weight o' ice forrard.' You
see, the ice on her bows were now a good six inches
thick, but Pete didn't say nothin'; 'cos w'y, there
wa'n't nothin' to say.

"Waal, that night, about midnight, w'en it were
a-snowin' so hard that we had to keep two hands
a-shovellin' it off the cabin skylights fur fear it'd
break 'em thro', the lookout sights a steamer, an'
the nex' minute she comes on into us ca-slap, bang,
crash! Fortunately the man forrard, as soon as he
hollered, jumped below an' pulled the fore-hatch
shut. The nex' second we wos all a-standin' on to
our heads an' bein' fired around the inside o' the boat
like there were a 'arthquack. Pete Murphy, wot
were a-steerin' o' the boat, we l'arned arterwards,
were picked up by the steamer, an' piloted her into
port. W'ich the same it were werry good; 'cos w'y,
he got his fee an' a purse from the passingers, wot
s'posed the rest o' us an' the boat was gone to Davy
Jones's locker.

"Waal, I wish you could 'a' seed the mix-up in
that 'ere boat. There were Bill Smock's rubber
boots in the cabin skylight along with a bag o'
'baccy an' Sam Sanders's Sunday shirt; an' it wa'n't
much o' a shirt arter that. I might also mention
that Sam hisself were standin' on his head in a cor-

ner on to Bill's plug-hat, w'ich the same it looked
werry much like a accordeen. An' Bill were lookin'
werry ord'nary, too. Hiram Pettybone, one o' the
best pilots on 'arth or water, had fell with his head
thro' the basin hole in a wash-stand, an' he were
a-hollerin' murder all he could. Pussonally, I were
in my bunk—that is, I were a-lyin' ag'in' the deck
over the same. We all made up our minds that we
wos a-goin' to the bottom, so we hadn't much to say,
'cept Hiram, an' he kep' right on hollerin'. Howsumever, arter waitin' some time, an' findin' we didn't
go down, we all commenced fur to pull ourselves together an' wonder wot were to be did. It didn't
take long fur to answer that 'ere question. We
could feel the wessel jumpin' like a porpoise, an' the
seas were a-breakin' over her deck—I mean her bottom—with a roar like thunder. Bill an' Hiram they
jess looked at each other, an' 'lowed that there wa'n't
nothin' to be did. We hadn't much more'n come to
that kinclusion w'en a tremenjous sea come an' rolled
the boat right over on to her beam-ends. We wos all
chucked about permiscus like agin, but Sam Sanders
he yells out:

"'Gee-whiz! I hope there'll be another.'

"An' sure 'nuff there were, an' it set the boat right
smack upon her keel agin. We all jumped to open
the hatches, an' we wos on deck mighty quick.
Waal, blow me for pickles, wot d' ye s'pose had happened?"

"What?" asked both boys.

"W'y, that steamer a-hittin' us had knocked all the ice off us forrard, an' we wos as clean as a whistle agin. But, my land sakes alive, how it were a-blowin'! W'y, the seas wos a-runnin' fully forty feet high, an' the rollin' an' pitchin' o' the boat wos enough fur to set you dizzy. The fust thing to be did were to get her canvas rejuced. By good-luck we wos right in the Gulf Stream w'en we wos turned over, so the water were warm enough fur to melt the ice in the runnin' riggin', an' we wos able to lower away an' reef the sails — that is, we reefed the mains'l. The fores'l blowed right out o' the bolt-ropes afore we could git to 't, an' w'en Bill sings out to me, 'Lower away the fores'l,' all as I could do were to sing back, 'Ain't no fores'l to lower.' Howsumever, she did fust-rate under a close-reefed mains'l an' a storm-jib. But there wa'n't no way o' keepin' the water out o' her now; 'cos w'y, some o' the deck seams had got started w'en the steamer run over us, an' the seas wos a-breakin' clean over her, an' so the water kep' a-flowin' right into her. We manned the pumps, but it didn't do no good. The water gained on us all the time.

"Waal, 'bout six hours later the mains'l blowed out, an' we had to set the storm-trys'l. The pitchin' an' rollin' wos now past all sense. W'y, she'd stand up so straight sometimes that the water inside o' her 'd pour out o' the cabin companion-way in such a stream that it nearly washed Bill Smock overboard. An' then she'd pitch down head-fust, an' that wa-

ter 'd go rippin' an' tearin' forrard so fast that steam
'd come out o' the deck seams.   One time we was
all afeard that the friction o' that water 'd set her
afire, but Sam Sanders he sez, sez he, the water 'd
put the fire out as fast as it 'd make it.   Towards
four o'clock in the afternoon she give a fearful lurch
over to port, an' then jerked back so hard to starboard that she rolled both her masts right out, an'
of course they took the bowsprit with 'em.   There
we wos, a dismasted an' waterlogged hulk in a hurricane.

"'Waal, by the great hook block!' sez Hiram
Pettybone, 'ef this wa'n't so blamed comic, it 'd
be gettin' ser'ous.'

"'We got to let her scud now,' sez Bill Smock,
sez he.

"So we ups helm an' lets her fall off till she got
right afore it. Waal, my goodness, how she did run!
She went so fast that the water along her sides were
all lit up with the phosphorus ; an' the water inside
o' her couldn't keep up with her, but kep' gittin' lef'
behind, so that it poured out o' the cabin hatch an'
ran overboard.   D' ye know, I've orfen thort sence
that were wot kep' her from sinkin'.   Annyhow, she
kep' a-goin' like a streak o' greased lightnin'.   Then
it come on to snow agin, an' she beginned fur to ice
up forrard some more.   Sez I to myself, sez I: 'This
settles it.   She can't float ef she gets iced up agin.'
Her head kep' a-gittin' lower an' lower, so that w'en
Bill Smock looked at it he putty nigh shook his head

"'EF THIS WEREN'T SO BLAMED COMIC, IT 'D BE GETTIN' SER'OUS'"

off. Howsumever, as I said afore, ye can't sink them
there bloomin' pilot-boats. Our boat were a-tearin'
along thro' the blindin' snow - storm, a-jumpin' an'
poundin' over the dreadful seas, w'en all on a suddent there were a frightful crash forrard, an' she
heeled over on her beam-ends agin. Wot ever d' ye
s'pose had happened ?"

" What ?" asked the boys, breathlessly.

" W'y, she'd run plump ca-bang bow on into a
iceberg."

The Old Sailor paused a moment to note the effect of this last statement, and then continued, im-
pressively :

"I sez to myself, sez I, this are the end o' the
whole business. But, bless ye, here I are a-tellin'
you about it, an' that are putty good proof that I
weren't drownded. Ye see, she'd gone an' run her
nose up on a part o' the berg wot were under water,
an' there she were stuck. Then Bill Smock sez he
to me, sez he, ' Go b'low an' see ef ye kin find anything fur to eat.' So I went down, an' blow me fur
pickles ef I didn't have to swim, the water inside o'
her were so deep. I reckon it must 'a' bin a comic
sight to see me a-swimmin' round an' round grabbin'
at boxes o' bread an' pickles an' things wot was
a-floatin' about. Howsumever, we got 'nuff to keep
us alive, an' that were all we wanted. Waal, the
nex' day the gale broke, an' we had nice weather.
We got right to work patchin' up the hole in her
bows made by runnin' ag'in' the iceberg, an' also put-

tin' a jury-rig on her, so's to keep her goin' w'en we got her afloat agin. We was putty much puzzled about gettin' her off, but good-luck saved us a heap o' trouble."

"How was that?" asked Henry.

"W'y, the warm water melted the ice out from under her, an' she floated off herself. Then we got her under way under the jury-rig, an' that very hour we sighted a steamer. But, d' ye know, the bloomin' lubber wouldn't let us put no pilot aboard. Yes, sir; she said we wosn't no pilot-boat, but a dirilick wessel manned by wrackers. An' so we had to sail our boat back to port with all hands aboard. But, bless ye, ye couldn't sink her!"

"It aren't a werry good day fur yarns," said the Old Sailor.

"Why not?" asked Henry, not understanding how one day could be more favorable than another for the exercise of the gentle craft of spinning "twisters."

"'Cos the wind are nor'east," was the reply.

"And what difference does that make?"

"It makes the difference 'tween rheumatism an' no rheumatism, an' w'en you has rheumatism in your leg, your head are not werry partikler about remem-berin' anything 'ceptin' words wot ort not to be said to a boy."

"Oh!" exclaimed Henry; and then he added, thoughtfully, "My mother has a liniment which will stop any ache that ever was."

"Does ye think as how she'd go fur to give some on 't to an old sailor-man?"

"I'm sure she would."

So they went to the house, where the painful limb was duly rubbed with the liniment, and the Old Sailor was seated in a big wooden arm-chair before the kitchen fire. There he gradually thawed out, and suddenly began thus:

"Pirates is not no good nohow you find 'em."

"Pirates!" exclaimed the two boys, eagerly; "did you ever meet them?"

"I've met everything wot floats, an' pirates floats, 'cos w'en they is on land we calls 'em land-sharks. But that ain't neither here nor there. Wot I war a-goin' fur to say to you air that pirates ain't no good, not even w'en they is gentlemen."

"How can a pirate be a gentleman?" asked Henry.

"Oh, it ain't no werry hard thing to be a gentleman," said the Old Sailor. "Leastways I 'ain't never seed no gentleman wot seemed to find it werry hard work. But, howsumever, moralizin' won't tell a yarn. W'en I war fust-mate o' the ship *Firebug*, bound from Boston to Calcutta, with a cargo o' hymn-books an' beans, I war about as well satisfied with my berth as ever any man could be wot had to work at all. She war a big, wall-sided hooker, were the *Firebug*, an' she carried a extry large crew, 'cos the owners wos smart enough to believe that she could make quicker passages if she wos well manned. Well, we got under way, and passed Minot's Ledge with a fine to'gallant breeze from the south'ard an' west'ard, all on a beautiful October mornin', an' we sings,

"'Good-bye, my Sally,
An' good-bye, my Mary Jane,
An' likewise Kate an' Molly,
Till we sees you all again.'

"I ain't a-goin' fur to waste your time an' mine
a-tellin' you how we got around Cape Cod, or how
we passed within a cable's length o' St. Paul's Rocks,
w'ich the same lays putty nigh on to the equator.
All in good time we weathered the Cape o' Good
Hope, an' got square up into the Injun Ocean.
Nothin' excitin' had happened to us up to that time,
'ceptin' a small gale o' wind, w'ich the same didn't
do no damage more'n to blow away the cook's apron.
It war a mean sort o' day now. The wind war
all in slants. Sometimes it 'd blow from the west,
an' sometimes from the south, an' sometimes it 'd
come in dead ahead an' take us all aback. It war
my watch on deck, an' I wa'n't in no werry good-
humor. All on a suddent the lookout sings out,
'Sail ho!' W'en I axed him about it, he said it
war dead ahead, an' about ten mile off. I didn't
think nothin' more about it till, an hour later, I noticed a werry smart-lookin' tops'l schooner about
four mile away, an' comin' down on us with a fa-
vorin' slant o' wind. I watched her fur a time, an'
made up my mind that she war a-goin' fur to come
within hailin' distance. W'en she got near enough
I brought my glass to bear on her to make out her
colors. I couldn't find no flag 'ceptin' at the fore,
an' there she carried a blue dove with a green branch
in his mouth on a white field. That would 'a bin a
good flag fur Noah or a peace society, but I couldn't
make out w'y a tops'l schooner should 'a bin a-carryin' of it in the Injun Ocean. It made me think
12

about a Christmas celebration wot I once seed—
Howsumever, that ain't got nawthin' to do with this
'ere yarn wot I'm a-tellin' ye.

"Well," continued the Old Sailor, "the schooner
comes a-sort o' driftin' down, an' byme-by I seed
that she carried several guns. So I sent word down
to the cap'n, an' he comes on deck an' takes a good
squint at her. Sez he to me, sez he, 'There's somethin' about the lines o' that craft I don't like, an' I
wish we had a gale o' wind behind us.' An' sez I
to him, sez I, 'Wot do ye make o' her?' An' sez
he, 'Pirates!' jess like that, him bein' cap'n o' the
ship. an' me fust-mate. Howsumever, it wa'n't no
use o' doin' anything, 'cos we couldn't. All we could
do was to 'wait dewelopments, as the hen said w'en
she sot down on the eggs. It war dead calm, an'
all that war bringin' the two wessels closer war that
queer kind o' driftin' wot allers do bring two wessels
closer together in a calm. Byme-by she war within
hailin' distance, an' then we got a ginuine surprise."

" Did they send a shot across your bows and order
you to heave to?" asked Henry, excitedly.

" No," answered the Old Sailor, gravely. "That's
the way they does in the story-books. No; the
skipper o' that 'ere craft appeared on the fo'c's'le
an' hailed us, sayin', 'Good-mornin', gentlemen, it
are a fine day.' Well, we couldn't hardly speak at
fust. 'Cos w'y? Nobody never seed such a skipper
afore. He had on a silk hat an' a Prince Albert
coat, a high collar an' a red necktie with a diamond

pin in it, a pair o' black-an'-white check pants, patent-leather shoes, an' kid gloves; an' blow me fur pickles ef he didn't carry a cane."

The Old Sailor paused, and studied the astonishment depicted on the faces of the two boys.

"You look s'prised at hearin' about it. Wot d' ye think we did, a-seein' of it? Well, the cap'n he finally mustered up sense enough to answer that it war a fine mornin' fur driftin'. 'Yes,' answered the other skipper, pleasant as a watermelon, 'we're werry good at driftin' ourselves. Wot ship are that?' An' the cap'n told him, an' axed him in turn who he wos. 'Oh,' he says, smilin', 'you'll be better acquainted with us in a few minutes. We're a-comin' aboard you.' 'Not ef I knows it,' said the cap'n. 'Keep off.' 'Oh, really,' says the dude cap'n, 'you aren't goin' to resist, are you?' 'In course,' says our cap'n. 'Oh, please don't,' says the other. 'Don't force us to usin' harsh measures.' An' with that he tapped kind o' thortful with his cane on a cannon. Our cap'n shook his head, an' sez he to me, sez he, 'Wot 'd I tell ye? Pirates, o' course.' Then the pirate cap'n he says: 'We're peaceful pirates, an' we don't like fightin' at all. We never shed no blood onless some bloody-minded sailor-man drives us to 't. We're a-comin' aboard you in a werry few minutes fur to see wot you got.' That's wot he sez, sez he, him a-standin' there on the rail over the gun, a-lookin' fur all the world like the smilin' willun in a drayma.

" Well, in a few minutes there come a breath o'
air that brought the two wessels together, an' then
fur the fust time we seed some o' the pirate crew,
fur they jumped on the rail to throw grapplin'-
irons. Blessed ef I ever seed sech a bloomin' lot o'
dudes in all my life. It were like bein' run aboard
of by Fifth Avnoo or Pickledilly. Them there
pirates wos all togged out in swell clothes, an' the
fust-mate wore a single eye-glass. An' they wos all
nice lookin'. They didn't look like ferocious pirates
at all. They looked like collidge stujents. Well,
we jess couldn't say a bloomin' word. All we could
do was to stand still an' hold our breath. To be
sure w'en their fust-mate come jumpin' down on
our deck, I did grab a belayin'-pin an' make a
move; but he smiles at me werry sweet, sticks a
little gold-mounted rewolwer under my nose, an' sez
he to me, sez he, 'I never pulled the trigger o' this
yet, an' I beg that you'll not compel me to do so.'
Well, I war all knocked silly, an' couldn't say
nothin.' The pirate cap'n he axes our cap'n wot
were the cargo, an' hearin' wot it war he laughs
an' says : 'Oh, indeed ! we really couldn't make
much use o' hymn-books 'cos we give up sich habits
years ago. We'll borrow a few beans, with your
permission. An' I think as how we could make
some use o' you an' your men, an' also your ship.'
Well, boys, our hearts went down into our boots
then, 'cos we smelt slavery in the air. I knowed
there wos some business o' sellin' white men to some

"'THEM THERE PIRATES WOS ALL TOGGED OUT IN SWELL CLOTHES, AN' THE FUST-MATE
WORE A SINGLE EYEGLASS'"

o' the savage tribes on the east coast o' Afrikee, an'
I guessed that were the line o' business o' this 'ere
pirate dude an' his crew. The pirate cap'n counted
our crew, an' he says: 'There's too many o' you fur
me to accommodate aboard o' my ship, so I'll keep
you aboard here. But I'll put half o' you in irons
below, an' let the other half help work the ship.
An' not bein' given to cruelty, I'll let the halves
change places every two days.' "

The Old Sailor paused in his narrative long
enough to note its effect on the two boys. They
were apparently impressed sufficiently to please
him, so he continued:

"As soon as the pirate cap'n had everything fixed
to suit him, he gave the orders to get under way,
an' a small bit o' a breeze havin' sprung up from
the nor'ard, off we goes east-sou'east. Our cap'n
war not acquainted with any land in that direction,
an' I'll say right here that there ain't none on any
chart. Howsumever, arter an easy sail o' thirty
hours we sighted land, an' in two hours an' a half
we wos at anchor in a werry neat bay on the south-
erly side o' a small island. The pirate cap'n now
told us that we wos at his home, an' he invited us
all to go ashore. Our cap'n an' me we kind o' de-
bated whether we shouldn't make a stand. 'Cos
w'y? We knowed ef we ever left our ship we'd
never git back to her. But the pirate cap'n smelled
a mouse, an' he sez somethin' to his men, an' they
all drawed gold an' silver mounted rewolwers an'

p'inted 'em at us. 'Gentlemen,' sez the pirate cap'n,
'please to go quiet, 'cos this time o' day my wife
allers takes a nap, an' ef we wos to shoot the noise
'd wake her up.'

"Well, arter them remarks, our nateral concloo-
sion were that we wos too bloomin' perlite fur to
go fur to disturb a lady. So we went ashore, an'
there we wos. The pirate cap'n diwided us up into
squads an' sent us off under charge o' warious pussons, all 'ceptin' our cap'n an' me. We wos took to
his own house, w'ich the same wos 'most too sweet.
W'y, the blessed pirate had a Axminster carpet on
his parlor floor, a white upright pianny, an' lace curtains at the winders tied back with white ribbons.
An' his wife war a putty little lady with yaller
hair an' blue eyes an' diamond rings. An' she war
a-sittin' at the pianny singin', 'O come to me, my
love,' w'en we walks in. She jumped up, an' sez she,
'Why, Willie, you got back real soon this time.'
An' he smiled, an' sez he to her, sez he, 'Yes, an'
I've got some gentlemen.' She smiled an' bowed
an' ran out o' the room. The pirate, arter axin' us
to sit down, sez to us, 'Gentlemen, by this time you
ought to know my name. It are William Quigg,
but I are generally knowed as Peaceful Willie, the
Daring Dove o' the Injun Ocean. I'm goin' to have
my history writ an' published under that title as
soon as I kin indooce some literary gent to wisit
me.' Then he went on to tell us that he perposed
to make the cap'n his body-servant an' me a sort o'

useful head man around the house. He said I could
boss the servants, an' I needn't be afraid o' their
leavin'. He got 'em the same way he did us. They
came along peaceful, he said, jess as we did. In
fact, it were the boast o' his life that he hadn't ever
killed any one or even wounded one. 'We've never
fired a gun from our ship,' sez he to us, sez he, jess
like that, him bein' a pirate an' we honest sailor-
men in captivity. He went on to explain to our
cap'n that a part o' his dooties would be readin' to
his new employer in the evenin's w'en he were at
home. He showed us his library, w'ich were full o'
sich books as, *Gettin' Everything in the World, How
to be Happy on a Million a Year, Get and Gather,
or Young Harlowe's Pluck, The Golden Harvest*, an'
the *Poems o' Martin F. Tupper*. I rubbed my eyes
an' thort I'd got into a Sunday-school library by
mistake.

"The cap'n an' me we didn't git no chance fur to
talk together fur two or three days, an' then we got
a half-hour. We spent a fair ten minutes a-wonderin' at the sort o' pirates we'd got took by. Then
the cap'n sez he to me, sez he, 'We got to escape
somehow.' An' sez I to him, sez I, 'Wot's the reason we can't get aboard their schooner some dark
night with our men an' run away with her? She's
armed, an' ef they wos to follow us in our ship we
could capture her an' carry both wessels an' the
whole pirate crew into Calcutta.' The cap'n agreed
that it were the right plan, an' so we set to work to

look fur chances to let our men know about it.
Well, it were a week afore we got our plan all fixed,
an' then we had to wait fur a dark night with a
favorable wind. The signal were to be the playin'
o' 'Home, Sweet Home' on the cap'n's flute, w'ich
the same he had been allowed to bring ashore with
him. Arter a few days the right kind o' a night
come along an' the tune were played. In half an
hour all our men wos on the beach, havin' sneaked
away from the peaceful pirates wot wos jess a-goin'
to sleep. We got off in a boat an' boarded the pirate schooner w'ere one man war doin' dooty as a
anchor-watch. We put him in the boat, an' told
him to git out. But of course he begin'd to holler
an' raise an alarm. Afore we could git the schooner
a-movin' off, Peaceful Willie an' a gang o' his dudes
comes alongside. 'Gentlemen, gentlemen,' sez he to
we, sez he, 'wot are ye tryin' to do? You wouldn't
go fur to leave us in this 'ere ongrateful way, would
you?' 'Yes, we jess would,' sez our cap'n, sez he.
'Keep off. I've got men at the guns an' others
armed with your rewolwers, an' ef ye try to come
aboard we'll blow ye into smithereens.' At that
Peaceful Willie an' his men all laffed. I got so
mad I yanked the lanyard o' a gun, but I jess broke
the string. I jumped to see wot were the matter o'
the gun, an' wot d' ye think?"

"What?" cried both boys.

"Them there guns wos wooden dummies! An'
w'en I tried to pull the trigger o' a rewolwer, it jess

sprung out a red fan. W'y, the bloomin' schooner were as peaceful as a suckin' dove."

"And so they boarded and took you back," said Henry, disappointed.

"Not much," exclaimed the Old Sailor. "We had the anchor up by that time an' some canvas on her, an' she gathered way. 'Get out!' yells our cap'n, 'or I'll run ye down an' sink ye.' 'Oh,' sez Peaceful Willie, 'you wouldn't do that, would ye, to a pirate wot never hurt no one?' 'Yes, sir,' sez our cap'n. 'Then we surrender,' sez Peaceful Willie. 'There sha'n't never be no bloodshed in my history.' So we took the whole kit an' crew aboard, incloodin' Peaceful Willie's wife, an' we set sail with both ships fur Calcutta. There we turned the Peaceful Pirates over to the police, who said they'd been the scourge o' them seas fur five years."

"Well," said Henry, "the captains of the ships they had captured must have been easily frightened."

"That werry same idee has occurred to me," said the Old Sailor, eagerly nodding his head.

THE Old Sailor sat looking out over the sea with a peculiarly pensive expression on his countenance. The two boys sat beside him gazing at him with deep anxiety. He had just made an astounding declaration, and it had filled his two young friends with mingled excitement and sorrow.

"Wot 'd you say," he had asked them, "if I wos to go fur to tell you that I war goin' to sea agin ?"

"You don't mean that you are going ?" cried Henry.

"That are edzackly wot I does mean."

"But why ?"

"'Cos there is some things I got to settle in my mind afore I kin rest ashore fur the balance o' my nateral life. I want to find out ef that there African king's darters has growed up civilized or cannibals. I want to go and see wot are become o' Thakelbolen's kingdom. I want to see ef I kin discover the Boyking Islands agin. I want to know ef that feller are still holdin' on to the north pole. An' most of all, I want to know ef the queendom o' Girlica are still runnin'."

"The queendom of Girlica!" exclaimed George. "What's that?"

"Didn't I never tell you 'bout that?"

"Why, no," said Henry.

"I told you 'bout the Boyking Islands, didn't I?"

"Yes."

"Well, the queendom o' Girlica are—but I'll begin at the beginnin' an' tell it straight. 'Cos w'y? This are the last yarn wot I'll go fur to tell ye afore I git under way fur furrin climes."

After pausing a few minutes to allow this statement to take due effect, the Old Sailor took a long look around the horizon, heaved a sigh, shook his head, and began thus:

"W'ich I hope I may never eat pie agin ef this 'ere wa'n't the werry identical way wot it happened. I were master o' the ship *Fried Clams*, bound from Philadelphy to Yokohama with a cargo o' Philadelphy ice-cream, scrapple, an' peppermint lozengers fur the Japanese department o' edication to use in edicatin' their women. We wos bound around the Horn fur the Pacific, an' we had good 'nuff weather till we got around there. Then it started in to blow, an' my cracky, but we got it in the eye! The seas run as high as the foreto'gall'nt-mast, an' the wind blew a hundred an' fifty-one an' a half mile an hour by actooal measurement. Howsumever, although the gale lasted fur six days, we rode it out without any ser'ous loss, savin' an' exceptin' the second-mate's red suspenders, w'ich the same wos car-

ried away the third day by reason of his fallin'
down the main hatch an' landin' in the scrapple.
But w'en the gale were over, we didn't know no
more about w'ere we wos than a bat in a coal-mine.
Ye see, the sky were still overcast, an' I couldn't
get no observation. On general principles, howsumever, I sot the course at nothe, an' let 'er go at
that. We hadn't bin a-runnin' on that course so
werry long w'en the lookout give the cry o' 'Sail ho !'
'Now,' sez I to myself, sez I, 'preehaps this 'ere ship
'll come nigh enough fur us to hail, an' we kin git
our reckonin' from 'er.' Sure 'nuff, we soon made
out that she were comin' that way. But w'en she
got near 'nuff fur us to git a good look at her, you
kin be sure we done some mighty tall starin'. My
sons, I've seed ships, an' ships, an' ships ; but I 'ain't
never seed one like that afore or since.

"Fust of all, blamed ef her sides wa'n't covered
with stamped leather, with figgers o' birds an' flowers an' all sich things all over 'em. The bowsprit
were painted w'ite an' gold, an' had a red scarf
twisted around it an' the ends hangin' down. All
along the top o' the bulwarks wos laid lace tidies,
an' in the deck ports wos brass boxes full o' flowers.
The sails wos all made o' different colored silks, embroidered with pink parrots, yaller elephants, blue
dogs, an' orange - colored ladies with brown faces.
The cabin were painted w'ite an' gold like the bowsprit, an' had a reg'lar roof-garden on top o' 't. Waal,
we stared an' stared, an' couldn't say a word. Byme-

"'YES; THE CAP'N WERE A WOMAN'"

by she come in hailin' distance, an' then her cap'n went up on the poop—I mean the roof-garden—an' hailed us. The cap'n had on a straw hat—wot folks ashore calls a sailor-hat—an' a blue monkey-jacket an' a blue skirt."

"Skirt?" cried the boys.

"Yes; the cap'n were a woman, an' the nex' thing we seed were that all the crew wos women. In short, the ship were manned by women—or ruther gals—ef ye kin say sich a thing. The cap'n sung out to us—an' it were reg'lar singin', too—to know wot wessel we wos an' w'ere boun'; w'ich the same, desirin' fur to be perlite, I answered. An' then she sez, says she, 'Wot's yer cargo?' Now, that wa'n't none o' her business; but still I didn' want to do nawthin' to hurt her feelin's, so I ups and tells her, 'Philadelphy ice-cream, scrapple, and peppermint lozengers.'

"'Oh, gals!' sez she, 'did you hear that?'

"An' they all 'lowed that they did. Then the cap'n, she sez, sez she:

"'I'm werry sorry fur to put you to any ill convenience, but we got to have that ice-cream.'

"'Young lady,' sez I to she, sez I, 'you can't git that ice-cream. It are for the Japanese ladies.'

"'Ladies, attention!' she cried. 'Aim an' turn on, please.'

"Then we seed 'em stickin' half a dozen hose-nozzles over the side at us, an' we laughed fit to kill. But the nex' minute we quit, I tell you. Them there

hoses squirted molasses all over us, an' in less time
'n it takes to tell ye, we wos all covered over with
the bloomin' sweet an' sticky stuff till we wa'n't fit
fur our own comp'ny. I hollered that I'd surrender,
an' I heerd the other cap'n say, 'Thank you, ladies;
that will do.' The squirtin' stopped, an' they lowered away a boat. It were manned by gals, an'
they rowed putty good too. The fust-mate o' the
other ship come aboard us. She were a red-headed
gal, an' had a mole on the end o' her nose, but she
knowed her business. She said as how she an' her
boat's crew wos to stay aboard o' us an' see that we
done wot we wos told. Our orders wos to foller the
other ship, an' a light breeze springin' up, we both
got under way. In two hours land were sighted,
an' in another hour we wos at anchor in a harbor
under the lee o' a werry big island, with mountains
in the middle.

"'Wot island are this?' I asks.

"'This are the Queendom o' Girlica,' sez the mate,
sez she.

"'An' wot are that?' sez I to she, sez I.

"'The land o' girls,' sez she to me, sez she. 'You
wait till you go ashore an' you'll find out all about it.'

"W'ich the same I done. The cap'n o' the putty
ship, w'ich her name were Hypatia Bock, she took
charge o' me. I s'posed, o' course, that I'd be took
right afore the queen; but Miss Bock, sez she to
me, sez she: 'Laws-a-massy, no! No men is allowed
to speak to the queen.' All the time she were a-talkin'

I seed she had somethin' in her mouth; but I didn't
ax no questions. 'Cos w'y? I had to wait till she
got through a-tellin' me about the queen. Wot she
told me were this: 'The Queendom o' Girlica were
a land w'ere women wos boss, an' men wa'n't. The
offices o' government wos all held by women an'
gals, an' men done the hired work. Furrin men wot
come ashore there wos held as slaves an' put to work
in the bakery.' 'The bakery?' sez I. 'Oh yes,' sez
she to me, sez she. 'We got a tremenjous bakery
here, an' it runs day an' night.' I sez to her, sez I,
'I s'pose you all must eat a drefful lot o' bread-an'-
butter.' 'Bread-an'-butter?' sez she. 'Do you think
we're a lot o' bread-an'-butter misses? I want you
fur to go fur to understan' that we don't eat neither
one.' 'Wot d' ye bake, then?' sez I. 'Cake,' sez she.
'We make more different kinds o' cake here than all
the other countries in the world put together. We
have different kinds fur breakfast, fur dinner, fur
supper, an' fur lunch afore we go to bed.' 'Wot
d' ye do about no butter?' sez I to she, sez I. 'Waal,'
she sez, 'we use molasses instead. Only the old
women have that. 'Cos w'y? W'en they gets to
be about thirty years old the cake don't taste sweet
no more, an' so they put molasses on to it.'

"'But,' sez I to she, sez I, 'they ain't old at thirty,
is they?' 'Oh, no woman ever gets to be more'n
thirty-five here,' sez she. 'How d' ye perwent it?'
sez I. 'Jess stop countin',' sez she. 'W'en we gets
to be twenty-six, we stays that fur five years, an' so

on. The men gets old, but we don't mind that.'
'Excuse me,' sez I, 'but would you mind a-tellin'
me wot it are you're a-eatin' of?' 'Oh,' sez she,
pullin' it out o' her mouth, 'that's my chewin'-gum,
o' course. We all chews it. There's a royal government factory w'ere it are made by tons, an' give
away free.' 'Free?' sez I. 'Oh yes,' sez she ; 'ef
the queen was to cut our chewin'-gum supply short,
we'd rise up an' yank her off the throne so quick
she'd never know wot hit her.' Jess then I seed a
large number o' young women goin' 'long the street,
an' they all had on the mos' tremenjous hats I ever
seed in all my born days. 'Wot's them?' I sez.
'Them's matinée gals,' sez she. 'They bin to the
symphony matinée at the music-hall.' 'Then you
has music, an' a band?' sez I. 'Sure,' sez she. 'An'
the conductor are jess too sweet fur anythin'. He
has the mos' beautiful hands in the world, an' his
hair falls right down to his waist, an' his eyes, w'en
he looks over his glasses, is jess heavingly.' 'An'
wot kind o' music do he give?' sez I. 'Oh,' sez she,
'symphonies an' things. But he are jess too sweet !'
'But w'y do them gals all wear sich big hats?' sez I.
'That's the fashion. The gal that kin wear the biggest hat without gettin' a sore neck from carryin' it
are allowed extra cake on Sunday nights.' I wondered how they carried them hats at all, but I didn't
say nawthin' fur fear o' offendin'.

"Nex' thing I axed her were wot they had in the
way o' intellectooal amoosements besides the music.

"'IT'S JUST TOO AWFULLY, DELICIOUSLY SWEET!'"

'Waal,' sez she, 'there's the dress debates.' 'Wot is them?' sez I to she, sez I. 'They is werry excitin',' sez she to me, sez she. 'Twicet a week,' sez she, 'we meets in the great public hall, an' the Lady High Chancellor presides, an' the Fust Maid o' the Chambers acts as secretary. We all sits aroun', an' looks kind o' uncomf'table till some lady sez she doesn't care, or somethin' like that, but she's goin' to have her nex' dress made with accordion-pleated insertion down the bias, an' leg-o'-mutton flounces.' Mebbe them wasn't her edzack words, but it sounded like 'em. 'Waal,' she went on, 'as soon as some one sez somethin' like that, then we all begins to talk at oncet about dresses, an' how we like 'em made, an' how we're goin' to, an' all that; an' it's jess too puffickly lovely fur anythin'. An' byme-by the menservants comes in an' passes aroun' cake an' molasses an' soda-water, an' then we goes home.'

" 'An' wot kind o' games does you have?' I axed her. 'Oh, lots an' lots,' sez she. 'There's cuttin' samples—that's a lovely game.' 'How d' yo play it?' sez I. 'W'y,' sez she, 'we're blindfolded, an' have a pair o' scissors. Then we're turned aroun' three times, an' started off. Wotever we run up ag'in' we try to cut a piece off fur a sample. Sometimes we cut corners off the lace curtains, or leaves off the plants; but wot we tries to do, o' course, is to catch some other woman, an' cut a piece off'n her dress.' 'But don't that spoil her dress?' sez I. 'O' course,' sez she, 'but then don't she have all the fun

13

o' goin' shoppin' fur another? But the finest o' all
our games are the game o' barg'in counter.' 'An'
how d' ye play that?' sez I to she, sez I. 'W'y, fust
of all,' sez she, 'we all dresses up in our walkin'
costumes, an' then we goes down to the great store-
house. The doors is kep' closed, an' we all crowds
aroun' outside tryin' to git in. The men inside set
out a lot o' goods on the counter, an' go to work
markin' down the prices. We kin see 'em thro' the
glass doors, an' we all gits excited. W'en they're
all ready they hangs up a sign, "Barg'in Sale," an'
throws open the doors. Then you ort to see the
fun! Some women gets knocked down an' walked
on, others has their dresses torn all to pieces, an'
others gits some o' their ribs broke. 'Cos w'y?
The game are to see who can git to the counter fust,
an' grab the marked-down goods. Interference are
allowed, an' sides are chosen sometimes. Anyhow,
six or eight women kin make a team an' work together. You jess ort to see me an' my three sisters,
each five feet ten inches tall, an' weighin' a hundred
an' seventy-five pounds each, git in line one behind
the other, an' butt our way through the crowd with
heads down. It's jess too awfully deliciously sweet,
that's wot it are!' 'W'y, that are a good deal like
football,' sez I. 'I don't know nothin' about no football,' sez she, 'but barg'in counter are the finest game
on 'arth.' An' her eyes flashed as she thort about it.

"Jess then a gal in a blue bonnet, with a gold
star on the front of it, comes along. 'That are the

Chief o' P'lice,' sez Miss Bock, sez she. The chief she comes right up to us, an' she sez, sez she: 'The queen's orders is that these 'ere strange men wot you've captured is to onload that Philadelphy ice-cream right away, so's it can be et with the cake afore goin' to bed to-night. Arter that they is to be taken an' sot to work in the chewin'-gum shops.' Then the chief walked away, swingin' her fan like it wos a club. Waal, I made up my mind that I'd got to git myself an' my crew out o' that country o' Girlica. 'Cos w'y? 'Twa'n't no place fur men. So right away I thort o' a beautiful scheme, an' sez I to Miss Bock, sez I, 'Ye mus' know that this 'ere Phila-delphy ice-cream wot I got ain't no plain waneller; it are tutti-frutti, that's wot it are, an' you'll find it putty rich.' 'Oh,' sez she, 'that are jess splendid.' Werry good. I goes off to my ship, an' I sot the crew to work a-puttin' the scrapple an' the pepper-mint-drops right into the ice-cream. W'en they got thro' it was the tutti-fruttiest ice-cream wot ye ever seed. Did them gals eat it? Waal, I jess guess they did. An' about the middle o' the night the entire female pop'lation o' Girlica were laid out with more different kinds o' cramps than any doctor ever heerd of. An' so, with the p'lice force an' the army so helpless they couldn't do nothin' but lay on to their backs an' kick, an' holler fur hot-water bags, I had nothin' to do but to steal boats, git my crew off to the ship, an' git under way. An' that were the last I ever seed or heerd o' the queendom o' Girlica."

www.ingramcontent.com/pod-product-compliance
Lightning Source LLC
Chambersburg PA
CBHW020113030726

47498CB00006B/2091